Praise for *Life After Near Death:*

"Life After Near Death is the latest, significant contribution to the previous work of a small group of guides. In a timely way, *Life After Near Death*, offers a very real confidence in the larger process because it exposes the fact that there is order, structure, and extraordinary intelligence and love that is actively influencing and shaping this Truman Show-like existence that dominates our human experience.

It's easier to have faith in the process and hope for the future after reading this good book."

—John L. Petersen,
founder and president of The Arlington
Institute and publisher of FUTUREdition

"This book is the culmination of the author's investigation into near-death experiences (NDEs) and focuses on the very important life changing after-effects which are all too easily overlooked. Following a spiritually transformative experience, the author herself developed newfound psychic abilities which enabled her to empathize with the experiencers that feature in this book. What gives this book a very unique perspective is that the author has used this ability to give readings for each of the NDErs that she interviewed. This gives a new and added dimension and perspective to the meaning of the NDE to these individuals. This is a very interesting book which leaves many 'pointers' for future researchers."

—Dr. Penny Sartori,
author of *The Wisdom of Near-Death Experiences*

LIFE
After Near
DEATH

Miraculous Stories of Healing and Transformation in the
Extraordinary Lives of People With Newfound Powers

DEBRA DIAMOND

NEW PAGE BOOKS
A division of The Career Press, Inc.
Wayne, NJ

LIFE AFTER NEAR DEATH

EDITED BY JODI BRANDON

TYPESET BY EILEEN MUNSON

Cover design by Joanna Williams/ Cover image by Yuri_Arcurs/iStock

Printed in the U.S.A.

To order this title, please call toll-free 1-800-CAREER-1 (NJ and Canada: 201-848-0310) to order using VISA or MasterCard, or for further information on books from Career Press.

CAREER PRESS   New Page BOOKS

The Career Press, Inc.

12 Parish Drive

Wayne, NJ 07470

www.careerpress.com

www.newpagebooks.com

Library of Congress Cataloging-in-Publication Data

Names: Diamond, Debra.

Title: Life after near death : miraculous stories of healing and
  transformation in the extraordinary lives of people with newfound powers /
  by Debra Diamond.

Description: 1 | Wayne : New Page Books, 2016. | Includes bibliographical
  references and index.

Identifiers: LCCN 2015038563| ISBN 9781632650245 (paperback) | ISBN
  9781632659743 (ebook)

Subjects: LCSH: Near-death experiences. | Death--Psychological aspects. |
  Parapsychology. | BISAC: BODY, MIND & SPIRIT / Parapsychology / Near-
Death
  Experience.

Classification: LCC BF1045.N4 D53 2016 | DDC 133.901/3--dc23 LC record
available at *http://lccn.loc.gov/2015038563*

✳ *Contents* ✳

❋ Preface ❋

Evelyn Carleton doesn't see the world exactly the same way as anyone else.

At age 36, Evelyn had a near-death experience that changed her life forever.

Evelyn had spent the day watching people get married at the Bahai Temple in Wilmette, Illinois. At the time, Evelyn was, as she said, "living life in the fast lane," working for a talent management agency as a single woman in Chicago. Alone at the Temple, Evelyn questioned her future and had concerns about her relationship with her boyfriend. Her life journey felt incomplete. That afternoon, Evelyn stood outside the Bahai Temple and demanded: "God, if there is something more, show it to me. I won't take one more step forward until you show me some answers."

Later that day Evelyn experienced her NDE (near-death experience), a result of a kidney stone that triggered a cardiac arrest, despite her being in perfect health up until then. She was rushed to the hospital

"Someone packed me with ice. I started going through a tunnel and left my physical body behind," Evelyn later said. "As soon as I was on the other side, I had no more pain." Evelyn encountered a white light and was given information about the mysteries of the universe. She was given the choice to return or stay but was then sucked back into her body. "Months later, everything I thought was important, seemed to mean nothing," Evelyn said. "I was different and knew I would never be the same again."

If that had been the end of Evelyn's story, it would be significant in itself, but the most profound events were yet to come.

Shortly after her hospital stay, Evelyn began to receive mysterious downloads of mathematical equations and quantum physics formulas.

Some unknown force spontaneously fed her these formulas and codes in an uncontrollable process.

Some years later, Evelyn heard about my research and contacted me to share her experience. When I spoke with her, Evelyn was desperate. She didn't understand the information, yet it kept coming. At that point, Evelyn was spending her days recording these codes and formulas—and had *32 binders of them.* For the last 20 years, Evelyn has compiled the formulas in notebooks, which she keeps stuffed in bins in her closets.

What do these codes mean? Are they the result of her medical experience? Psychosis? A neurological condition?

Following her experience, Evelyn moved to Texas and worked as a personal assistant. Today, she lives alone in a garden apartment, is semi-retired, and wonders what she is supposed to do with her gifts. Will Evelyn's formulas be deciphered by scientists? Will they someday unlock a great mystery?

Tony Woody was a 24-year-old Navy flight engineer with top security clearance when he was involved in a near-fatal collision in a training jet. Shortly afterward, Tony was awakened in the middle of the night and found himself transported to another dimension. He witnessed a bright light and geometric shapes that were more than three dimensional, no two the same. Tony had the urge to merge with the light. The love he felt was unconditional and he knew it wasn't a dream.

"It's so overwhelming, it takes you over," he says. "These experiences were the most real experiences that ever happened to me."

Following the event, Tony stayed awake staring at the residual energy, the glowing white light. "What was I supposed to do?" he said as he recounted his story and the unexpected miracle to me.

Afterward, Tony had many questions: Who am I and what am I becoming? Why did I have this experience? Tony spent years looking for the answers—studying spiritual principles and religions including Christianity, Sufism, Zoroastrianism, and Buddhism in hundreds of books. Eventually, Tony concluded the answers lay outside the boundaries of religion or theology.

Although Tony has a degree in IT, since his experience he's been unable to use a computer; computers reboot or crash when he's nearby. His physical proximity causes gas station pumps to malfunction and he can't even wear a watch. His sensitivity has become paramount, beyond the malfunctioning of ordinary equipment. His son, who was only 2 1/2 and asleep in the next room at the time of Tony's experience, is now 26 and he, too, is unable to wear a watch to this day.

What happened to Tony? Why does he experience this electrical sensitivity that causes machinery to malfunction? What did he rub shoulders with in his experience? And what is it about the place that Tony traveled to that seemed more real than reality itself? Was Tony switched "on" in some unique way?

✳✳✳

Jessica Haynes was a 27-year-old art gallery manager in Carmel, California, when she was in a horrific car crash and sustained life-threatening injuries. Her doctors didn't think she would recover or ever walk again.

Until the accident, Jessica had dedicated herself to her work and her boyfriend. Life was difficult and she felt unable to exit the constraining box her world had become.

Following the accident, the rest of Jessica's life crumbled: She found herself out of a job. Her boyfriend left her. Her face was disfigured, the vertebrae in her spine crushed, and the bones in her feet shattered. She couldn't move below her waist and her pain was excruciating.

"I'm dead," she thought as she lay in a bed in her hospital room.

During her NDE, Jessica found herself in a dark place as waves of energy rolled over her. She experienced aspects of her childhood and career over and over again, and was shown alternate ways she could live her life going forward.

Within six months, Jessica was completely recovered from her accident—so much so that she was running long distances, although she was supposed to be in a body brace for a minimum of six months. Today, Jessica is a happily married artist living a complete life in Northern California.

What happened to heal Jessica completely? Was she somehow chosen for her experience because she needed a second chance at life? Was her NDE the key to unlock her body's self-healing power? What was Jessica delivered back with that was so much greater than what she possessed prior to her accident?

Ordinary to Extraordinary

Like millions of others, Evelyn, Tony, and Jessica had near-death experiences—*life-changing events that made them re-examine their lives.* More importantly, these three didn't just return with a new outlook. Each of their brushes with death left them with extraordinary gifts. Special powers. Completely new abilities that did not exist prior to their NDEs. These ordinary people had become extraordinary.

All three returned from their near-death experiences with specific cognitive, physiologic, and psychological *after-effects.* After-effects of an unprecedented scope. After-effects that are permanent transformations. These experiencers' after-effects produced radical changes in their lives, including an array of talents, gifts, and skills they had no inkling of before. These after-effects turned them into people unrecognizable from their former selves.

What happened to Evelyn, Tony, and Jessica to endow them with seemingly superhuman powers? Though these three received remarkable properties, not every NDEr receives these specific after-effects. Some receive other properties, such as chemical sensitivity or sensitivity to light, and psychological after-effects, like enhanced spirituality or profound love for humanity.

Life After Near Death

What you'll find in *Life After Near Death* are profiles of a dozen individuals whom I interviewed, from a universe of about 50 people with NDE after-effects. Each has what I call "near-death experience after-effects." These after-effects don't discriminate. The individuals range widely in age, location, socioeconomic status, religion, and professional background. They span in age from their 20s to 60s, from unemployed to accomplished professionals, from the East Coast to the West Coast and abroad. They include men and women. There's a former CEO and scientist who, after nearly dying, compulsively makes art for months at a time; a cyber-intuitive who communicates with machines; a therapist whose IQ rose to MENSA level; and a college professor whose eyesight corrected to better-than-perfect vision.

Over a period of three years, I crisscrossed the country interviewing these men and women, trying to uncover the meaning behind their near-death experiences and after-effects. These stories are real, and the experiencer's names are included with their permission, with the exception of three people with pseudonyms: Evelyn, Marissa, and Lyla. Diverse as they are, these people share a transformation—one that has been, for many of them, as complex, mystifying, and entangled as the near-death experience that initiated their journey.

Like these individuals, I was mystified the first time I encountered a near-death experience, and I immediately wanted to understand it better. Probing the experience left me with more questions than answers. After interviewing these NDErs, a number of coherent themes emerged to uncover a deeper understanding of the phenomenon beyond the experience of the individuals who have them. And now, I bring this information to you.

Most books on the afterlife revolve around questions such as "Will I see my loved ones again?" and "Will I meet God or my spiritual teacher?" However, those questions are just the beginning of what I discuss in *Life After Near Death*.

Life After Near Death examines the stories of a dozen individuals who came back from their experiences transformed. Yet, it is also the story of all of us and our relationship with the universe, reality, and consciousness. *Life After Near Death* helps us understand the essential energetic nature of the universe to shed light on what all our lives are about.

That is the story I present here. It's not easy to explain the mysteries of the universe. You do not have to believe this, but I trust it to be true.

Life After Near Death is broken into five parts. In Part I, I explore my background and basic definitions of the NDE. In Part II, I examine stories of people who have experienced miraculous transformations as a result of their NDEs. In Part 3, I step back and examine the reality of the NDE and questions about how experiencers deal with its aftermath. In Part 4, I explore more complex cases of near-death after-effects. And in Part 5, I examine the implications of the near-death experience for all of us and our planet.

✳ Introduction ✳

What is a near-death experience? A delusion? A neurochemical imbalance? Or the result of a dying brain? Or is it something else—something ineffable, a journey to an indescribable realm that can transform and forever alter the experiencer?

Raymond Moody coined the term *near-death experience* in his groundbreaking book *Life After Life* in 1975, in which he outlined nine elements of the NDE, including a life review, an out-of-body experience, encounters with deceased loved ones, and a decision to return to one's body. Eight years later, Bruce Greyson, a professor at the University of Virginia, expanded the list to encompass 16 elements, including a sudden insight, experiencing scenes from the future, and arriving at a point of no return.

According to most NDE literature, common elements of an NDE include an out-of-body experience, a feeling of peace with the universe, a sense of profound love, and a connection with a brilliant white light. (Appendix A provides a complete list and definitions of all the elements of an NDE.)

Regardless of the common elements, a lack of consensus of a single definition of the near-death experience still exists. Entire lifetimes can be reviewed, deceased beings met, and gifts given all within seconds or minutes of earth time. The emotional intensity of an NDE is unlike any other experience a person can encounter on earth. Yet so much about the NDE remains unknown.

Most people think you have to "die" and then "come back" to have an NDE. You don't need to be declared clinically dead to experience an NDE, although many near-death experiences are the result of accidents, heart attacks, and similar events that are often, but not always, fatal.

Also, it's not necessary to experience all of Moody's nine elements, or even more than a handful, to have a near-death experience. According to ACISTE (American Center for the Integration of Spiritually Transformative Experiences) and IANDS (International Association for Near-Death Experiencers), the key is not how many elements you experience, but rather that you return *permanently transformed* following the experience, unable to return to your former life. I agree with these definitions of the nature of NDEs.

NDEs are not uncommon. According to a 1992 Gallup poll, approximately 13 million Americans report having experienced an NDE. The number could be even higher, since many decline to discuss the experience out of fear of ridicule and embarrassment.

How Does Science View the Near-Death Experience?

What does the scientific community have to say about the near-death experience? Are NDEs a byproduct of hyperventilation? The result of diminished oxygen or decreased blood supply? Or is there a supernatural explanation for the phenomenon?

Science continues to greet the matter of the NDE, indeed psi (all matters parapsychological) with a healthy dose of skepticism. According to current scientific thinking, the near-death state is a delusion caused by hypoxia (reduced oxygen) to the brain, resulting in hallucinations. Experts believe the brain shuts down within 20 to 30 seconds after the heart stops beating, and once that happens it's not possible to be aware of anything. Current thought claims there is no basis for the belief that we survive physical death.

Yet, even as science expresses skepticism, more and more experiencers are stepping forward, with testimonials on YouTube and personal appearances on *Dr. Oz* and *Today*. It appears to be time to re-examine the meaning of the NDE and, indeed, how we consider death and the afterlife.

As I began down the path of exploring the NDE, I set up my process as outlined in Appendix II, leapt into the uncharted, and began my work.

NDE After-Effects: What Are They?

I was intrigued by the NDE realm, but it was the after-effects that fascinated me.

NDE after-effects—the lingering behavior that remains once the NDE is over—are permanent transformations that are even less well understood than the NDE itself. These after-effects have not been widely researched and, in our nomenclature, are often viewed as modern-day miracles. NDE after-effects can be disturbing and disruptive. Not every experiencer has the same after-effects. Just as each NDE is unique, each version of after-effects is unique.

Some experiencers return to life with traits completely foreign to them or supernatural gifts, such as enhanced cognition and unconventional sensory abilities. Some of these are expressed as compulsions. Many after-effects have no outlet for expression on earth, such as enhanced chemical sensitivity or the ability to know what complete strangers are thinking or feeling. NDE after-effects have consequences in many realms, from cognitive and physiological to social and psychological.

Social and psychological after-effects, such as increased spirituality and enhanced psychic ability, are difficult to measure and verify. I quickly moved beyond those after-effects to examine the more tangible cognitive and physiological gifts—abilities that could be measured and verified. Although all of the after-effects call for more investigation, the cognitive and physiological aspects, which had not been closely examined, required greater probing. I was particularly interested in these, as they are irrefutable and demonstrable.

Cognitive and Physiological NDE After-Effects

Cognitive and physiological near-death after-effects not only manifest as unusual talents and abilities, they may become obsessions that completely take over an experiencer's life. To be clear, what I am referring to is not a simple matter of banging out a few keys on a piano or occasionally picking up a paintbrush to dash off a watercolor. Experiencers with these after-effects become totally focused on their newfound abilities, often to the exclusion of everything and everyone else. Experiencers Dan Rhema (see Chapter 6) and Ana Callan (see Chapter 15) cannot turn off their flow of inspiration. It interferes with their lives and their day-to-day existence. A greater force—the power beyond the physical—has taken over. Experiencers are transformed into artists, writers, musicians, and mathematicians following their NDEs.

Physiological after-effects are even more bizarre: enhanced hearing, improved vision, burgeoning IQ, robust athletic ability, spontaneous healing. Some after-effects are truly frightening and can be dangerous, such as increased electrical sensitivity. These after-effects should not to be regarded as a panacea or the long-sought-after answer for a stalled life. Know this: *NDE after-effects come with a hefty price tag.*

NDE after-effects are mostly an interference, an intrusion that may require a complete re-ordering of one's life. They may require old habits, jobs, and lifestyles to be jettisoned in favor of unbidden abilities that are not always adaptable into practical, everyday living.

Near-death experience after-effects are a field in which little data exists. I was comfortable with that and with researching this field since, in my former profession, I pulled together, researched, and synthesized disparate pieces of information in areas that were not well understood. I researched industries and companies that were so early, they weren't even cutting edge. That was my experience, and I was able to see things and connect the dots in a way that others couldn't.

Plus, I had always been a hybrid, according to those I worked with—and the "bell cow," the one out in front of the herd. That was me.

The research I did into the field of NDE after-effects was modeled on the pick-and-shovel work I had done for many years. As I moved into the world of NDE after-effects and identified experiencers with cognitive or physiological after-effects, I utilized a methodology based on this past work that included a combination of conventional and psi research. (See Appendix B for a further explanation of the methodology.)

My Desire to Write *Life After Near Death*

My own interest in the spiritual realm was a result of a profound experience that led to a shift to a more metaphysical life. Prior to this shift, my life was limited to the material world as a mother and Wall Street executive. My shift—a transformative experience, but not in a situation near-death—led me to make use of my unique skills and background. Eight years ago, my personal life and career, marked by exemplary but conventional success, were irrevocably altered. I had a spiritual experience that left me as a clairvoyant. This was not something I asked for, nor something I was seeking.

In this "otherworldly" experience, I found I could see and communicate with people who had passed over—and because I had no experience with this sort of thing, I was frightened. As my life unfolded, it gradually dawned on me that I was dealing with a power that was not conventional. I evolved from a reluctant initiate into the world of spirituality to begin to train to make use of the gifts I'd been given. More meaningful coincidences occurred as I waded deeper into the world of spiritual exploration and this ultimately resulted in my work in the NDE realm. My work naturally evolved into a practice in which I combined my background with my spiritual abilities.

Whereas my initial goal in this work was to probe the after-effects of the near-death experience, very quickly events—sometimes unintended yet deeply meaningful to me—led me in different directions. These included a weightier examination of the deeper meaning behind the NDE and aspects that had been largely ignored or given short shrift by other seekers. And the results yielded something amazing—larger perceptions stunning in their scope and complexity. I encountered the complex ideas of consciousness and intent as I explored the prism that is our reality. Narratives emerged that included the smaller stories of the NDErs, which evolved into larger insights and a contemplation of the role of the universe in all of our lives.

This has been the most important work I've undertaken. I know there are doubters, and if I were sitting in your chair, I'm not sure I would believe this. A story turned into a deep journey into the ethereal, despite its unlikely genesis in a classroom near Penn Station in New York City some eight years ago. If someone had told me my life would be turned upside down and become completely unrecognizable, that I would undertake research into the NDE realm, I wouldn't have believed them.

At times in this work, I felt as if I was passing through a deep cloud bank or juggling water. Yet, I also realized that I had an opportunity to use my abilities to bring distinct knowledge to others. After all, death and the afterlife are matters that concern all of us.

My Background

1 ✳ *My Introduction Into the World of Spirit* ✳

"The most beautiful experience we can
have is the mysterious."
—Albert Einstein

I thought about the events that led me to where I was. I'd come a long way.

I was born in Ohio and spent most of my youth there. Mom was an elementary school teacher and Dad was an entrepreneur. I was a good student, on the honor roll, and enrolled in college when I was 17, graduating after three years. I received a master's degree at the age of 22. I was always on the fast track. A reporter from the *Baltimore Sun* once said, "Being early—sometimes very early—has been the story of Mrs. Diamond's life," in a feature article about me.

After I received my MBA, I was hired as an analyst for an investment firm. For 20 years, I was a busy person, with 10 balls in the air all the time, a husband, and three kids. I didn't have time to sit down and philosophize and sort it all out. By then, I'd had a successful career on Wall Street investing and doing commentary on CNBC. I'd done many things: venture capitalist, served on boards, helped companies start businesses, and mentored others.

When I was in the investment business, I realized I had a leg up. I knew things. It was a knowing that came in instantly. I took it for granted that I had good intuition and I was involved in a career that involved intuitive hunches. That's how I explained it: good intuition. My boss used to say, "Debra, you have good instincts," and I decided that must be the answer. I didn't know how else to understand it. No part of the Wall Street vocabulary included New Age vocabulary. Although you might hear "Go with your gut" or "What do your instincts tell you?" there's no place for spirituality in this dollars and cents business.

I didn't tell anyone that I knew things—how an industry might grow, how a company was going to do, what a management team was like. I encountered skepticism my first few years in the business, but after a few years of me being ahead of the pack, others began to listen. They would scratch their heads and say, "We don't know how you do it, but keep going." I was referred to as "an absolutely gifted investor, with remarkable intuitions."

A New York Classroom and a Visit From the Afterlife

In 2008, I had a spiritual experience that left me forever changed. As a way to gain context for that, I began to study energy work and developed a practice. In the process, I began to "listen" for my clients and have used my abilities since then in a variety of ways.

I've always had an interest in developing my intuition and thought it would be fun to learn a few tricks to tune it up. A workshop in New York on intuition development seemed interesting when it first came to my attention, but every time I considered signing up, something else came up. Now I know: I wasn't ready. When we're ready, Spirit puts it in front of us. Finally, the time seemed right, and I signed up for the class in November 2008.

It was a weekend class in Midtown Manhattan near Penn Station. *This will be fun*, I thought. *I'll get in touch with my senses, learn to trust my hunches—the inklings we all have.*

Twenty-five students were in the class, which included men and women. Some had experience; others were novices. The teacher was an academic who had written several books on spirituality and Eastern religion. I relaxed as we began our work. We practiced a few exercises in mental telepathy, learning to communicate without the use of sound or visual clues and kept things light.

We had been working for a few hours, practicing meditation techniques, when we took a break. I was surprised when we returned and the class took a different turn.

"Now we're going to do a séance," the teacher announced.

A séance? *No way. This is not what I signed up for*, I thought as I looked at the class description. Calling in the dead? I thought this was an intuition development class. New mindfulness techniques. How to tune in to your gut. Maybe a few exercises with cards.

I couldn't escape. I was a member of the class. *Well, I'll just do it and that will be that*, I thought. *Nothing's going to happen anyway.*

"I'll tell you what to do if you see someone," the teacher offered. I watched and listened as she explained that if a person who had passed over appeared in the corner of the room, they were probably associated with an individual seated in that corner. If we saw someone, we should ask if anyone in the class could identify that person. *Interesting*, I thought, *but not relevant, since I'm not going to see anyone.* I figured we'd do this and then move on to the next exercise.

My idea of a séance was pretty limited. I imagined blowing trumpets and the class seated around a table in a darkened room. Perhaps there would be some rapping. I looked around for a crystal ball. Nope. We were just in a dingy classroom on the eighth floor of an office building.

The teacher explained how we should approach this. There was a procedure to it. *Okay*, I thought. She said she'd put us in a meditative state and if we saw anything, to let her know and she'd help us. *Fine. I'll meditate and then we'll move on to the next exercise*, I decided.

I closed my eyes and listened as the teacher sent us into a relaxed state. I slowed my breathing and listened to her instructions to relax my body and soften my heart. I felt my head drop to my chest and I slumped in my seat. I was relaxed but aware that my back was sore from sitting in the straight-back chair.

I felt a few light sensations but quickly dismissed them. I was warm, which I attributed to the room. (It was a warm day in New York and the teacher suggested we keep the windows closed since the street noise may bother us.) I felt a slight tingling. The earth didn't shake. The room was silent. Nothing out of the ordinary happened.

And then the teacher said we could open our eyes. If we "saw" anything, we should let her know. I sat up.

"Did anyone 'see' anything?" she asked.

I looked around the room. All the students looked at each other. No one raised their hand. I raised my hand.

"Yes, Debra? What do you see?" she asked.

"I see about 50 people," I said.

Everyone gasped. I would have gasped, too, except I was busy looking at my brother's niece, who had passed away a year earlier. She was sitting on a white fence and looked happy. A white pony was beside her. (She had been an equestrian.) In the corner of the room, a man with a handlebar mustache flashed me a broad smile. A football player caught a pass in the middle of the room. My aunt was laughing up a storm in front of me. There were others I did not know, including 42nd Street showgirls prancing through the center of the room. A pushcart peddler crossed in front of me.

Everyone looked real. It didn't register to me that I was looking at people who had passed over. They all seemed eager to talk. Only later did I fully realize these individuals were not alive.

The teacher asked me what I saw.

When I described the man with the handlebar mustache and the broad, white smile, a woman in the corner began to sob. She spoke up and identified the man as her fiancé, who had passed away two years earlier. The teacher asked if he had any message for her.

I said I would check, even though I didn't know exactly what to do. I asked if he had a message and he said, "I died."

"He died," I said. (I have to say I've gotten much better since then.)

The woman in the corner continued to cry. Later she asked if she could show me a picture of her fiancé during our break. She had pictures on her cell phone. Could I identify him?

"Sure," I said, never doubting that I could do that.

At the break, she flipped through her pictures.

"That one!" I said, pointing to a man with a handlebar mustache, dark hair, and a broad smile. "That's him!"

She began to cry again. She had wanted to hear from him since his death and said she was now at ease, knowing he had communicated with her. She gave me a big hug and thanked me. I helped to facilitate a contact she so badly wanted. I helped her in a meaningful way.

I stopped to consider this.

I had done something important. I had never done anything in my career on Wall Street that elicited that kind of response. In the investment business, your job is to outmaneuver the stock market, outthink other strategists, or outperform the averages. It's all about the money. Helping someone is not part of your mission.

Life would never be the same.

A New Way of Life

Despite the rewards, I hadn't asked for this ability and was not seeking it. I called one of my sons on my way home to Baltimore that Sunday night. I have three sons, but this particular one is very skeptical and always scores high on logic tests. I related the story of what happened in the class. He didn't say a word and didn't interrupt. When I was finished, he said. "Well, that makes sense. We're just energy, and the energy has to go somewhere."

His explanation put my experience in a context I could understand, although I was still bewildered by the events.

I didn't tell anyone what happened that weekend. Most of the people I knew worked on Wall Street, and none of them would have understood or believed me. They would have rolled their eyes or, even worse, laughed at me. I didn't want to look crazy, so I kept quiet.

I can't let my life go in this direction, I resolved. *I have to control this.*

A boomerang had been launched at me. I tried to dodge it, but somehow it stuck anyway. There was no going back.

Was I crazy? I didn't think so. Had I done anything to provoke this? Was I making it up? My mind sorted through all the possibilities. How would I go on with my life now that this door had been opened? Did I pretend it didn't happen? Shove it behind a curtain? I couldn't.

I am a down-to-earth, practical person—a hard-nosed businesswoman. I find the idea that I am defined as a psychic uncomfortable. This wasn't something I ever considered for my life. It was not something I dreamed about or wanted.

I'm not ready for this.

I tried not to think about it, but somehow it's not that easy.

That summer, I decided to leave Baltimore—my home—to visit Taos, New Mexico. My plan was to paint there for two months.

Two years later, I was still there. That's not uncommon for Taos. When you meet the locals and ask how long they've been there, they say, "Oh, I came for a weekend—20 years ago." For artists, creatives, and spiritualists, the place exerts a magnetic hold.

In Taos, I relaxed about what happened to me and who I was. Without even realizing it, I began to accept it.

It was time, Spirit decided, for me to work with this energy. I relaxed and gave a nod to Spirit.

I began to train, take workshops, and study under practitioners, including teachers at the Arthur Findlay College in the UK. I was starting to grow and learn about my strengths as I made my way in this new world. My intuition, which had hastily departed after the experience in New York—driven away by fear, returned. With some distance and perspective, I realized I didn't see making money as an end-all and be-all for my existence.

Without this initial thrust into the world of Spirit, I would have remained a smart business lady focused on making money. I would not have examined near-death experiences and nothing in my life over the past eight years would have transpired. I was thrust into the world of spirituality with all the subtlety of a cyclone.

Life After Near Death describes the events as they occurred to me and as I experienced them as I was led into the world of the NDE. I wrote this story as it unfolded. No longer did I spend my days placing orders for millions of dollars or listening to the latest takeover rumors on Wall Street or leads on hot IPOs. No longer did I attend extravagant cocktail receptions, jet overseas to meet clients, or attend conferences in exotic locales. Instead, I used my talents to explore unanswered questions that concern all of us.

I became comfortable with my new gifts as the years passed. In Taos, when someone asks what you do, and you say, "I'm a psychic," they say, "Me too!" It was okay to do this work—at least for the time being.

Several years passed and I became part of the Taos community. I had my writing group, my knitting group, and my volunteer work at SOMOS, the literary society. I made many wonderful friends, people very different from the money managers and analysts I knew in my former life. The East Coast seemed very far away.

Taos served as a kind of dividing line between one life and another. I evolved from a reluctant initiate into the world of spirituality to make use of the gifts I'd been given. Since then, I've done readings, taught workshops, and been a speaker. My work is focused on helping others. If, 10 years ago, someone had told me that I would be doing this work, I never would have believed them.

Just as I knew there was no turning back from settling in Taos when I first arrived, a few years later I recognized my time in Taos would be ending soon.

Would I put the world of Taos behind me? Would this be the finale of my journey into the metaphysical life?

Before I left Taos, I decided to journey with a Shaman in Santa Fe on an inner quest to retrieve information from an unseen dimension—a type of spiritual consultation.

On the Shamanic journey, I was shown my childhood: a young girl who would not be coaxed into anything—who always chose her own path. I was shown a map of the United States, and in particular a city in the Southwest. I didn't know where the city was—or even which state— but I knew it wasn't New Mexico, California, or Texas. The city was lit up like a marquee. I sensed that Spirit was trying to show me something, even if I didn't know exactly what it was. I filed the information away, reminding myself to pay attention to clues about this unknown destination.

A few months after the Shamanic journey, I returned home to Baltimore. I spent my time writing and painting, catching up with friends, and visiting my family. Soon I was approached by a woman who had "died" at 36 from a cardiac arrest and came back to life, baffling her doctors. She had heard about me and asked if I would read for her. It was a traditional reading, not an NDE reading, and soon other readings followed. Before long, through word-of-mouth, I was reading for others, many of them professionals in the Mid-Atlantic.

The months passed, I was busy, and winter arrived. The clear, crisp air and the mysterious, penetrating nighttime darkness of New Mexico were in the past. It was gray and damp in Baltimore. I'd had it up to my eyeballs with the cold. I'd read about the Tucson Gem and Mineral Show, which takes place each year in February. Pleasant days in Tucson beckoned.

Why not? I thought.

Going Deeper Into the World of NDEs

Soon, I packed my bags. I planned to add a few tools to my spiritual tool box and enjoy Tucson's sunny skies and temperate winter.

I arrived at my hotel in the Catalina Foothills, the dry air warm against my skin. As I unpacked, my cell phone vibrated with a text message from a friend. I looked down.

Do you know Dr. Gary Schwartz, a prominent scholar at the intersection of science and spirituality?

I Googled him. Gary Schwartz received his PhD from Harvard and was director of the Yale Psychophysiology Center and the Yale Behavioral Medicine Clinic, prior to moving to Arizona to do research at the University of Arizona's Veritas Laboratory. Dr. Schwartz conducts investigative research using mediums to demonstrate Spirit's role for guidance.

Gary Schwartz sounded interesting, like someone I would enjoy meeting one day.

I uncapped a bottle of water and opened the *Arizona Daily Star*, the Tucson daily newspaper, and stopped. There was a full-page announcement: Dr. Gary Schwartz would be speaking the following evening at the Unity Church about a mile from where I was staying. The room was warm and, as I fanned myself, I thought about the chances of that coincidence.

Not likely, I concluded.

The next night I sat in the front row of the Unity Church as a breeze ruffled the colorful flags in the sanctuary overhead. I listened as Dr. Schwartz presented his evidence about proof of Spirit. At the end of his presentation, another speaker stepped forward and made an announcement. The next evening there would be a meeting for the local near-death experience group. *Why not? I'll go to that, too.*

The next night I was back in the chapel, listening as Dave Bennett explained how he had been a commercial diver 20 years earlier, when he drowned on a job. While "dead," he peeked into the future and experienced a paradigm shift. Later, Dave discovered he had stage-four cancer, from which he fully recovered. I listened as he explained his experience. I was intrigued. After the presentation, I exited the church into the warm February evening and thought about what I heard. There was more to this near-death experience, I was convinced.

As I drove down Speedway Boulevard the following day, cutting through the swath of mountains that ring Tucson, I thought about near-death experiencers. Wherever these experiencers went during their NDEs, I knew I went there, too. I had seen it. Tasted it. I shared something with them. We were all travelers to that unseen realm.

With that, my entry into the realm of the afterlife was kick-started. But its true arrival wouldn't take place until months later back on the East Coast.

Moving Into the World of the Near-Death Experience

Six months later in Baltimore, a friend mentioned that the International Association for Near-Death Studies (seems like they have associations for everything these days) would hold their annual meeting in Washington, DC. They needed healers to volunteer. "They could use you," she said, and I agreed to help out.

A week later, I drove past Arlington Cemetery, down Jefferson Davis Highway, to Crystal City, a suburb of Washington, DC, where the conference was being held.

The Marriott was bustling, the halls crowded with groups huddled in conversation while others scanned the day's schedule or waited in line to enter a workshop. I was told to report to the "healing" area.

"I'm here to volunteer for healing," I told the man behind the desk.

"We don't need any more healers," the man said.

Great, I thought.

"I'm also a psychic," I volunteered.

"Okay. Write that down on a sign-up sheet and we'll see if anyone signs up," he muttered.

Within a few minutes a man came by for a reading. When I was done, he thanked me and left.

Five minutes later the man was back. "Now you're going to read for _____." He mentioned the name of a man, a well-known professional. Not only did this individual have a brush with death, but he came back from his NDE with special artistic gifts. Months later I would replay that moment over and over in my head.

"Don't you know who he is?" the man insisted.

"No," I answered.

He told me this man had been struck by lightning and came back from his near-death experience with special abilities.

Okay, I thought. *That's fine.* Not much shakes me up. I'd held meetings with Fortune 500 CEOs, done interviews on CNBC, and hosted my own radio show. I could roll with the punches. So I noted this information and just kept going. The man arrived for his reading and settled into a chair while I pulled up one across from him, and we got started.

I put my head down, tuned in, and concentrated. After all, it was just another reading.

Except it wasn't.

When I began to read for this man, I realized this was no ordinary reading. This time, the information I was shown (psychics are shown information in symbols) was literally out of this world. Symbols from the universe. Galaxies. Stars. Foreign materials outside our realm. Abilities to transcend our reality. This man's brush with death left him with extraordinary gifts, with special powers. This was no ordinary man.

In the days after the reading, I continued to think about what I'd been shown. The reading started a train of thought and questions: How did this individual develop these after-effects? What was he supposed to do with them? Why him? What about other NDErs? Did they receive gifts, too?

The questions were endless. I Googled "near-death experience after-effects" and found that little research had been done.

It was going to be up to me to answer the questions.

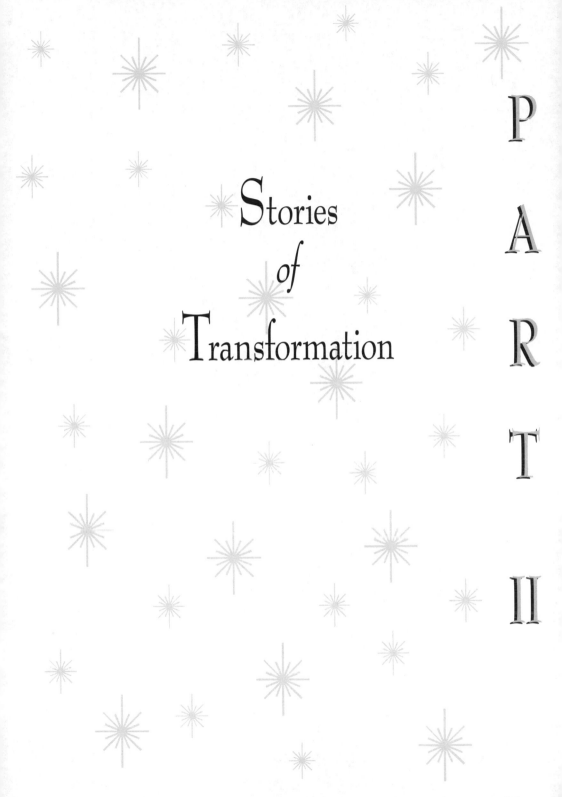

Stories
of
Transformation

PART II

2 ✳ Javier Pereza and Physiological Transformation: ✳ Newfound Athletic Talent

"The real secret of lifelong good health
is actually the opposite: Let your body
take care of you."
—Deepak Chopra

In 2013 I decided to head to the West Coast to attend UCLA's writer's program. In the fall I moved to LA to set up shop, attend classes, and begin to delve into the world of the NDE more deeply.

I settled in to a cute apartment in Santa Monica, expecting to spend time polishing up my writing and sizing up the NDE realm. I looked forward to a change—if only for a short period—beautiful weather, and classes that would expand my knowledge about point of view and style, all while meeting new people. Soon enough, though, I found out the universe had other plans for me.

The World of the NDE Opens Up in California

It was a typical, perfect sunny day in Southern California. I headed south on the I-10 to Orange County, on my way to a local IANDS (International Association for Near-Death Experiencers) chapter meeting in Tustin.

A week earlier, I received an email announcing the meeting. An experiencer would be speaking and there would be time for socializing afterward. I was looking forward to it.

It was an ideal opportunity to hear my first story. I turned off the Santa Ana Freeway toward Tustin, as I thought about the person who asked me to read for the professional in Crystal City. He lived in Southern California and it crossed my mind that I might see him at the meeting. *Nah. That would be too weird.*

The Unity Church parking lot was packed as I pulled in, squeezing between a Toyota and a Honda. I crossed through a public garden to a small room where a group of about 30 people were seated in folding chairs in what appeared to be a children's classroom. It was a sunny September afternoon, but the air was chilly, and I shivered as I pulled my light jacket tighter around my shoulders.

As I turned to scan the room, I noticed the man who suggested I read for the man in Crystal City standing behind me. We hugged and I explained why I was at the meeting. *A sign?*

Once the meeting began, the group was anxious to hear from the new experiencer, who had never spoken about his case in public before. The room was packed with curious onlookers and rubberneckers, fascinated by the topic of the afterlife. Regulars chipped in with anecdotes about the metaphysical community, updates on new cases, and news for the day's meeting.

Javier, the new experiencer, told his story briefly. Javier experienced many elements of the NDE: an out-of-body experience, heightened alertness and consciousness, encountering a bright light, and an alteration in time and space. Javier returned from his experience permanently transformed, although his experience did not involve physical trauma. Like others I would meet, Javier returned altered, with permanent after-effects. This was important information to note, as I met other experiencers who entered the realm through a different mode.

The room burst into applause when Javier finished his story. Everyone was thrilled about his presentation and his decision to "go public."

The meeting lasted three hours, with a break for snacks and coffee, followed by a happy hour at a local restaurant where the group kept the conversation going. Javier didn't join the group at the restaurant, but we made arrangements to meet and discuss his case further. I couldn't help but be intrigued by what I had heard.

As I drove back from Tustin to LA, my mind wandered. As I got closer to the city, I took in the amazing view. I could actually see the LA skyline. As I passed the Getty Center, I thought about how it seemed I was following a path, as if river stones were laid out, one by one, in front of me. Winding up in a meeting in Tustin, California, with a man who was responsible for igniting my interest in this topic seemed more than a coincidence.

The next day I wanted to ask Javier other questions. It had been seven years since his experience, but he was still eager to talk about it. I emailed him and he emailed me back with these responses:

> I simply went to sleep one night and at the precise moment that my 92-year-old grandmother passed, 4:11 am March 31, 2006, I had my experience. At the end of my experience, everything went black. I felt like I entered the eternal void. Like nothing ever was or will be. That sensation still lingers today and hits me every few weeks. That's when I feel disconnected in time and space, when I feel for two or three seconds that I'm in limbo again.
>
> After that experience, I couldn't stop crying and the next morning I couldn't get out of bed.

I glanced further down the email. Javier mentioned his upbringing.

> I was the lightest skinned child in an Hispanic household, which according to Hispanic tradition, made me the favorite. I was also a tyrant. When I wanted to eat, the whole family ate. When I wanted to go on vacation, we all went on vacation. I was also my grandmother's favorite.

And that's where the story gets interesting. I read on.

> I had not been in touch with my family for two and a half years. The following night after my NDE, the phone rang. I instinctively said, "And there it is!"
>
> Sure enough, it was my closet female cousin, Elizabeth. Her first words were, "I am so sorry to bother you, but I have some bad news."
>
> I immediately interrupted her. "It's okay, I know Grandma passed away."
>
> "Did one of your brothers already call you?" she asked.
>
> "No, Grandma said goodbye last night," I told her.

I reread Javier's responses to the questionnaire I sent him, noting the elements he listed and his after-effects, including new, heightened talents. I knew there was something more going on than meets the eye, and I wanted to know more about his experience.

Javier and I agreed to meet at my apartment for a reading the following week. He seemed excited and was interested to see what we might learn.

Javier's Session and His Newfound Physical Abilities

I looked out the window and watched as a dark-haired man dressed in a polo shirt and light khakis got out of his car. Javier. He looked boyish with his cropped hair and compact physique, but I guessed he was in his 30s. A few minutes later the doorbell rang.

I opened the door, and Javier walked in and took in the small room as my cats scurried under the bed. The living room was decorated with a sunny green couch and colorful IKEA prints. It was dominated by a large flat-screen television and a panel of windows along the side wall that flooded the room with bright California sunshine.

"Nice place," he said. I gestured outside, toward the perpetual sunshine, the busy shopping street below and said, "Yes, I love it here."

We chatted about his experience, from which he was still recovering. The first seven years had been rough, and he'd had difficulty incorporating the experience into his life. He had finally reached a point of peace and acceptance, and was ready to unpack what had happened. I offered him a coffee, but he shook his head and said he preferred to get started.

I gestured to the chairs and table I had pulled into the middle of the room for our session. We took seats across the table from each other as I explained that I would spend a minute getting into a meditative state.

"I'm in a state of concentration," I said, "but you can interrupt and ask questions." Within minutes we began the reading.

I took a few deep breaths and as I began, I immediately noticed Javier's aura, the energetic field that surrounds the physical body. His aura was unusual, and I saw something I had not seen before.

"Your aura is not like most people's," I said. "The first layer, closest to your body, is almost completely black." This close-in aura represented

Javier's physical aura, his physical life on earth. Javier's life had been mired with difficulties; the black represented the hard times or trauma he had encountered.

"There's more?" Javier asked.

"Yes. There's another layer beyond that, which is completely violet and white. This layer is light-filled and it extends outward from your body," I said. "This outer aura covers up your dark aura."

Through his experience, Javier appeared to have gained a new layer of spirituality and resilience represented by his new light-filled aura. A newfound layer of protection, gratis of the universe.

I mentioned to Javier that I was also shown a curious symbol that I had never seen before: a man inside a circle and a square—a man with multiple levels of spirituality, almost like a hologram. I realized quickly this was Vitruvian man from DaVinci's drawing—a blend of art and science. (I'm an artist and trained in art history.)

I understood this symbol to indicate that Javier's experience had blended two worlds: the world of Spirit and the world of science. Vitruvian man demonstrated that Javier had encountered two distinct realms that seldom meet, and Spirit was showing me that intersection.

"This man is not an ordinary person," I told Javier. "He is multi-dimensional."

Javier's experience itself was a like a type of hologram. Like a hologram, Javier's experience encompassed shifting vibrations and perspectives from a light source that was no longer present.

We continued the reading as I asked: "What happened to Javier in his journey?"

Javier was transported to another realm, where he encountered a higher frequency. This higher frequency, this new charge, allowed him to absorb otherworldly sensations, imbuing him with new behaviors when he returned, Spirit said.

Javier returned with new sensations and abilities. For seven years, he tried to cope and live with the changes he was dealing with. He knew he had changed. He not only encountered another realm, he encountered another energy—one we don't encounter on earth.

But we wondered: Why did Javier's experience coincide with his grandmother's passing? What was the significance of his grandmother's passing to Javier's NDE?

When Javier's grandmother passed, through her determination, and the tremendous energetic force she produced as she passed, she pushed through a message that was important that her favorite grandchild—Javier—receive. The strong connection between Javier and his grandmother was necessary for the connection to be made.

That link—that energy, I would find in other cases—suggested that consciousness survives the physical body, that energy can be directed and focused to transmit information and messages from other realms.

Javier's Transformation

Javier was a self-proclaimed narcissist in a dead-end, paper-pushing job prior to his experience. After his NDE, Javier's life was transformed. Now Javier shows concern for his co-workers, his family, and his parents, making sure his parents have everything they need as they age. He drives them to Costco and throws birthday parties for his nieces and nephews. Javier has a new career writing radio scripts and has been promoted to a managerial position.

Javier was altered after his experience. His transformation included a cerebral shift and, more importantly, a physical shift. Javier has become athletic. Prior to his experience, Javier never played sports; never wanted to participate. He never played any competitive sport until he was 37, four years after his experience. On his days off prior to his experience, Javier would sit at home and watch documentaries. Now he plays softball, pushing his physical body as if he's in training for a marathon. In a way, he is— his marathon for a new life.

Here is what Javier managed to accomplish in his first year of playing sports:

Javier plays in a national, well-organized baseball league that utilizes formal rankings for all its players. Javier went from being rated a 6 to a 10 (out of a possible 11). He was originally considered a new, unskilled player and assigned the lesser position of catcher. He was later moved to the more critical and demanding position of left fielder.

He was consistently told that he is a "natural" and that he must have begun playing in his youth. His team was shocked to learn that he only began playing at the age of 37.

His ability grew exponentially. He went from being unable to catch any ball of any kind (pop-ups or grounders) to hitting many grand slams.

Javier was given the "Best Offensive Player" trophy. "I never dreamt I would ever achieve any athletic recognition of any kind in my lifetime," he says.

Athleticism was never on Javier's radar. It was simply not anything he considered for himself. Now, it's an important part of his life, one he makes time for no matter how tired he is.

Javier emailed me a picture of himself from his youth. A young boy with thick glasses, dark, shaggy hair, and a quiet expression peered back at me—about as far from a "jock" as one could imagine.

For the work ahead—the extra effort his life now requires—Javier requires more exertion and greater fortitude. His work and commitments mandate that he be physically stronger. Javier now works non-stop, helping his parents and his relatives, pursuing his career, and staying on course to be of service.

Javier couldn't understand why he had become an athlete after an entire lifetime spent passively watching documentaries, as an introvert. As we examined his new mission and his new priority to serve others, he understood his newfound physical readiness was a way for him to be in training, to build stamina for his work ahead.

Javier explained the sort of person he used to be: "I was very low energy. I had enough energy to go to work. Go to school. But I barely had enough energy to meet someone for coffee. I was very quiet and I liked to stay home a lot."

"What about now?" I asked.

"Now, I meet people for lunch. I go places after work. On weekends I play softball. My brothers are all in shock. They don't recognize me," Javier said. "I don't recognize myself."

I nodded. "It must be confusing," I added, considering his more active life.

"It's funny because every time I feel overwhelmed, I get this message: *There's a lot more to go. You've got to keep going.*"

And keep going he does. Javier must keep his body in shape for the life he now leads, his mission-driven, active life.

"What does your family think about your transformation?" I asked, wondering how he was handling those who might be skeptical of his shift.

"When my friends or family ask if I'm trying to be the good son, I say, 'No. It has nothing to do with that. Don't get it twisted.' I tell them I'm not trying to be the good son. It's just something I do now." Javier calls his life an "after-school special."

I looked into Javier's life now. Here's what I found:

Javier's been imbued as a messenger of spiritual light. His body is being used to accomplish his work here on earth. There was a purpose to Javier's experience, a purpose that encompasses all of us. Javier has work to do as a beacon of light for the universe, Spirit said.

And he must be physically strong to accomplish his mission. The old Javier would be a non-participant. Now he is out there competing, becoming physically stronger, and making sure his team is winning. This activity brings rewards to Javier but to others, too.

"Yes, that's how I physically feel. Like I'm giving everyone a nugget of energy," Javier told me.

We wondered, what caused Javier's shift?

The energetic plane that Javier experienced possesses unique tools at its disposal. The energetic tools of light, velocity, and powerful effects. These are not tools we recognize on earth. These are metaphysical tools which are condensed, supercharged forms of energy. They are phenomena meant to grab our attention to be forever imprinted on our consciousness.

Javier came back from his experience transformed, literally. He doesn't look the same, act the same, or think the same way he did before.

He leaned forward and looked at me. "I've only recently accepted that. It's not scary anymore."

Needing Time to Change and Accept

Javier has profoundly changed since his experience, having only recently reached a place where he is able to process his NDE, and embrace it philosophically and emotionally. But we can't discount that it took him seven years filled with emotional and psychological challenges.

Yet, despite the positive elements, Javier's experience itself was not filled with love, joy, or happiness. Parts of his experience were harrowing and shocking, like when he was shown a montage of figures that were terrifying and he had the sensation of being pricked by thousands of sharp needles.

"I only recently accepted that I wouldn't be the person I am today if this had been a positive experience," Javier said as he shifted in his seat.

We asked: Did Javier encounter a divine realm in his experience?

Javier stepped into a heavenly realm for just a second, long enough to lift up the scrim, to show him he was not meant to be there. Almost like he walked into the wrong room. And then he was told to leave.

"Yes. That's exactly how I felt: Wait! I'm in the wrong place," Javier said.

Now that Javier is back, he is not always sure where he's supposed to be. Despite adjusting to this life-altering experience, much of him is still spiritually "out there." He wonders if the two realms will ever merge?

Javier and I concluded the reading. He seemed calm—at peace. He confirmed the reading cleared up some of his questions.

Javier Follows Up

Later in the day, I heard a buzz and looked down at my cell phone. I had a text from Javier: "Here's a weird 'coincidence.' I found this image online after your email 'prompted' me to search for it."

It was a picture of Vitruvian man. The caption underneath it read "Vitruvian Man Inside Tunnel."

Why was Vitruvian man inside a tunnel? I wondered. *Was this the tunnel of the NDE? Was DaVinci himself an experiencer at the intersection of science and the Cosmos?*

Like other geniuses (Galileo, Michelangelo, Newton, and others), DaVinci had talents and knowledge for which we have no explanation—gifts that were decades ahead of their time. Gifts that produced miraculous advances in art and science, and progress in blending the two. We don't know for certain, but can speculate that perhaps these brilliant artists and scientists had some type of noetic experience, one that gave them a peek into the universe as well.

Javier thought that was the last chapter of his book, but he was wrong. Rather, the door has been opened for him and it's not going to close. Javier will go on with his life, but in a different way—a new way meant to bring light to all of us. His enhanced strength will give him the capability for his work ahead. Every once in a while, he'll get a reminder that he's been forever transformed.

3 ✳ Barbara Whitfield and Physiological Transformation: ✳ Electrical Interference

> "Is it a fact—or have I dreamt it—that, by
> means of electricity, the world of matter has
> become a great nerve, vibrating thousands
> of miles in a breathless point of time?"
> —Nathaniel Hawthorne

I was learning that New Age work was almost mainstream in California. Many experiencers were interested in examining their spiritual experiences. When people asked what I was doing in Santa Monica and I mentioned I was researching NDEs, they'd say, "I've had eight of them," or something similar, even if they hadn't had a single one.

When Barbara Whitfield, a woman who once lived in Baltimore, contacted me about this research, I made arrangements to interview her. She mentioned she lived in Baltimore long enough to "pick up" her then-fiancé and move to Atlanta. She was eager to participate in the work and responded quickly to the questionnaire. Barbara has been around the NDE world for 30 years and worked with others in this small world of researchers, as an assistant to both Kenneth Ring and Bruce Greyson, early founders of IANDS (International Association for Near-Death Experiencers).

I took one last look at my notes. I would be reading for Barbara that afternoon. I imagined what she looked like based on my correspondence with her. Vivacious, dark hair, full of life, a broad smile, and an upbeat personality.

I reread her explanation of what happened to her as I reviewed her notes. She wrote:

I was suspended in a circle bed after spinal surgery in 1975 at age 32. I was on a ventilator for 20 minute treatments and the ventilator failed to reverse.

45

The air continued to flow into my lungs but the mouthpiece was "stuck" so I couldn't push it out. That was when I left my body and found myself in the hallway outside my room.

I pictured Barbara's spirit hovering in the hospital corridor, as her body lay inert in the hospital bed down the hall.

When she left her body in her NDE, Barbara entered a tunnel, which she described as an "otherworldly realm." There she met her grand-mother, who had died 14 years earlier. Together, the two of them reviewed Barbara's life.

One of the more interesting aspects of Barbara's NDE was the conversation she was able to overhear at the nurse's station when she was out of her body. I placed a sticky note on her questionnaire to include a question about this in her session: How was she able to hear the nurse's conversation when she was physically in another room?

Barbara's Session: A Lesson in Electrical Sensitivity

I looked at my watch: four o'clock. Time for Barbara's reading. She'd be done babysitting her granddaughter. I pulled up a chair to my laptop and dialed Barbara on Skype. She answered on the first ring. With her youthful energy and dark hair, she looked at least a decade younger than her late 60s, when I peered at her through the computer screen.

We chatted about the weather and the questions, and then Barbara warned me. "I'm very electrically sensitive. I blew out my car battery and I've been blowing things all week," she said. "I'm just warning you."

Electrical sensitivity was one of the NDE after-effects I was interested in. I'd heard about lights that flickered on and off when NDErs entered a room, computers and electronics that malfunctioned, light bulbs that exploded, watch batteries that died. These seem to happen most frequently when a high-anxiety situation was present, when the NDEr was emotionally stimulated, excited, or upset.

I took a few deep breaths as Barbara and I began the reading. I would be focusing on the specific events that happened to Barbara in her reading, much as I did in Javier's reading (see Chapter 2). I turned on my recorder as Barbara watched through the laptop screen. I was ready to begin.

Exploring Consciousness in the NDE

Barbara began by asking about her life review:

"It seemed as if I was able to feel every emotion of my entire life during my life review. How was this possible?" (Barbara remembers the experience vividly, even to this day, 30 years later.)

Here's what Spirit had to say: *Our consciousness absorbs everything during our lifetime. Yet, consciousness occupies a realm of no time and no space. There is no past, present, or future as far as consciousness is concerned. When we are in our earthly bodies, we cannot fathom this since our earthly bodies experience events sequentially, linearly, through our physical senses. This creates our reality. Yet, when we are free of our physical body, we experience hyper-real perception and ultra-clarity. Our consciousness is able to register everything happening in the universe with total clarity unencumbered by our physicality.*

"That makes sense," Barbara said, "but what was the energy I encountered and merged with during my NDE?"

Here's what Spirit showed me: Each of us has our own individual consciousness. Think of it as a chip that resides within us. It is our essence when we're on earth. This consciousness separates when we leave our body, yet continues to exist, independent of our body. When our consciousness leaves, it merges with the collective consciousness. Barbara's consciousness connected with collective consciousness during her NDE. This connection granted her instant knowing, a connection with everything and everyone, in all time and all space. *Our consciousness has the ability to exist, absorb, record, and process in this other reality, this alternate plane of existence*, Spirit said.

When I glanced at Barbara, she was nodding along with me.

I paused for a moment to consider this information concerning the survival of consciousness. This was the first time I was shown (in an NDE reading) the ability of our soul, our essence to "know" outside of our physical bodies. Spirit was communicating directly to convey this concept of the survival of consciousness and I made note of it.

Spirit continued: *Consciousness is the most minute fraction of everything. Space does not exist in consciousness. Yet consciousness takes up everything, everywhere. It is as far and vast as we can imagine. And beyond that.*

47

Barbara eyed me through the computer screen and I gave her the thumbs up. We chatted for a few more minutes and then agreed to move on to the next question, which concerned her upbringing.

I already knew, both from speaking with Barbara and through her answers to the questionnaire, that she had experienced abuse and emotional trauma in her past. Did her underlying biology trigger anything about her NDE? It was an important question, and her answer might provide a deeper look into the type of person who was a candidate for this experience.

"Let's ask if your underlying biology or upbringing triggered your NDE," I suggested. Here is what we were told:

People who have emotional trauma are more malleable, as if there's a "switch" that's waiting to be activated. Some part of Barbara had already been softened up prior to her NDE. This made her more open and ready, somehow more connected to the experience. In a sense, Barbara was waiting to be triggered. Her childhood abuse, her emotional vulnerability, primed her for this event. It made her a candidate, a willing participant to exit this plane and experience another more beautiful, more complete reality.

"Well, there is," Barbara said. "We have a switch. That switch is easier [for those with a past like mine, Barbara implied] and we also have the ability to let go. The trigger was there for me."

I cleared my throat and reached for water. It was beginning to get dark and the room was growing dim. I turned on a lamp next to the table.

"Can we maintain the frequency of an NDE on earth?" Barbara asked.

"Why do you ask?"

"I wanted to stay there," she said. "I've tried to replicate the experience here but I can't."

As I would later learn, other experiencers would voice the same desire and concern. It's something they yearn for but can't quite achieve.

Spirit said: *Our earth bodies are too heavy to experience that entrance to another plane. Our consciousness needs to be completely separate from our physical body to experience that frequency. When our consciousness is connected to our body, we are too dense to experience the Universal All.*

In other words, no.

Where Is the Realm of the NDE?

When Barbara left her body during her NDE, she went to another realm. Where was that realm? Was it heaven? Was it the afterlife?

It was a realm of all existence. Of all time and space yet of no time and no space. A realm of all beings. It contains all the answers we don't have and all the thoughts to pose of our existence. We're not capable of forming the correct vocabulary to access this realm, Spirit told me.

For Barbara's essence to end up outside of her body, her consciousness needed to be catapulted with a considerable force through a confluence of physical, emotional, and spiritual events. The timing had to be right. At the time of her NDE, Barbara's life was in crisis, her marriage was not going well, and her physical body was traumatized from surgery. The combination of these events and the ability for her to accept and enter an alternate reality converged at that exquisite moment, and the universe appears to have interceded.

Because she hadn't experienced all the elements of the NDE, Barbara had some lingering concerns. She had not seen a white light, for example, so she wondered why she'd been deprived of that. Certain elements of the NDE have received so much attention and been so strongly allied with the NDE that when an NDEr does not experience every element, or even any of the elements, they believe their experience must not be valid. Barbara's question was a good one, because she, too, wondered if a missing element hinted that somehow her experience wasn't complete.

I took another breath. This is what we learned:

The white light did not need to be part of Barbara's experience. Like others, Barbara was shown what she needed to know. Barbara had a life review and an out-of-body experience. She met her grandmother. Her NDE left her profoundly changed and affected. Not everyone experiences each element, but each individual experiences what they need to, in the most effective way for them to maximize the event and its outcome.

The universe knows what it is doing, tucked up behind the scenes, it appears.

A doorbell rang at Barbara's house. I stopped talking and looked up at the screen.

"Just ignore that," she said. "My husband will get it."

Ready to continue, I put my head down and took another deep breath.

"What is the ball of light that others see?" Barbara asked.

As we pass through the doorway into infinity, the ball of light is our collective essence, the entry to universal consciousness. It is there to greet us. The light is our collective relatives, our souls, our ancestors, all who have come before us. All that has existed and lives in infinity, that continues to exist, that powerful and iconic symbol of everlasting Spirit.

"Yes," Barbara said. Then she murmured something to someone at her home before turning back to me.

When experiencers like Barbara encounter interruptions in their readings, it stops me momentarily, but it does not interrupt my connection. It's almost like taking a station break or watching a commercial during the regularly scheduled program. I don't have any trouble picking up where we left off when we resume. We continued as Barbara went on to the next question.

"Why did I meet my grandmother during my life review?" Barbara asked. "She passed 14 years earlier, yet she was there in my NDE."

Barbara's life review was meant to be a mirror held up to her consciousness, Spirit said. *Everything was reflected on it and from it continuously, as if it were a giant mirror ball that rotates and reflects light in many directions all at once. Like a mirror ball, Barbara's consciousness consists of millions of facets, each a mirrored surface gathering information, processing it and sending it back. Consciousness is not only able to take in what is happening in any particular moment, it is able to absorb a lifetime continuously, refracting, reflecting, and retaining all events. All events, past, present, and future take place at once in higher consciousness.*

Barbara did not have to process the information through her cognitive senses, which is why it was received and acknowledged so acutely. This information would come up in other NDE readings as well, I would learn.

And her grandmother? Why did she deliver Barbara's life review?

Barbara's grandmother was the person most likely to influence Barbara in her life, which was why she was the one to join Barbara and deliver her life review. Her presence would be most meaningful and most likely to impress the NDE on Barbara.

"What was I meant to learn from my NDE?" Barbara asked.

Most experiencers wanted to explore this question, which was uppermost in their minds. This is what we were told:

Like others, Barbara was meant to spread the light, to align with the energy of the universe and to distribute that energy on our planet as a catalyst for the light.

Was Barbara Selected for Her NDE?

Like Barbara herself, I was curious if she was selected for her NDE? Was she somehow a candidate for this extraordinary experience?

Spirit told us that Barbara had certain qualities that could make her a missionary on earth. Compassion and the ability to empathize made her suitable when certain events and her earthly time line aligned. As someone who had experienced trauma—both physical and emotional—this made Barbara yearn for an alternative existence at the soul level.

Trauma appears to be one of the prerequisites for NDE candidates—people who have reached a point where their life is referenced by darkness. Yet they have the ability and the desire, whether conscious or not, to enter the light. And for many, this is exactly what happens following their NDE.

Barbara remarked that her current work as a therapist and thanatologist (someone who works with the dying) would not have happened if she hadn't experienced an NDE. Like Javier, Barbara attributes her life today to the NDE. Her life has completely changed and she has been transformed since the experience—into another person, one unrecognizable from her former self.

"The memory of my NDE was the most vivid and clear event of my life." Barbara said. "Why, after all these years, is the experience so exceptionally memorable and sharp?"

Barbara's NDE was the most profound event of consciousness of her existence. The only time in her life she would meet universal consciousness. The only time her consciousness would be completely separate from her body, aside from death. The only time she is able to experience absolute clarity, undiluted by physicality or earthly interference. The event remains permanently imprinted on her consciousness and brought back as clearly today as if it happened five minutes ago.

Consciousness doesn't get old. It's the same age when you're one as when you're 90. It's always the same age. When you pass, consciousness continues to live, to take in information and interact, but from a higher plane of existence, Spirit said.

We also wanted to know what brought about the end of Barbara's NDE? We asked, why did it end when it did?

Barbara's experience was complete. All that needed to be accomplished, was accomplished. Barbara was shoehorned back into her body when it was over. The process of rejoining her body was inelegant since merging consciousness back with a physical body is difficult. Even though consciousness is not a physical thing—it's fine and air-like—it's weighty in terms of its existence. Putting that huge living thing back into an earthly body produces a significant jolt.

All the NDErs I interviewed remarked on this "jolt," the impact at the conclusion of their NDE as they re-entered their bodies.

I asked Barbara how her life changed since her NDE. "My life is totally different now," she said referring to the fact that she divorced her husband. "I tried for nine years to get my husband [her childhood sweetheart] to accept my changes and he couldn't."

Like other NDErs who divorced, Barbara's former spouse said, "Honey, if you'd only stay the way your were, we'd be fine."

But NDErs can't stay the same. It's impossible. Barbara eventually remarried and considers it a healthy relationship. Today, she and her second husband write and teach together. Barbara also returned to school to become a therapist.

There it was: that change—in lifestyle, profession, personal circumstances, and learning to deal with the after-effects of the NDE and the new reality of life on earth.

At the end of our session, I thanked Barbara. She was with me throughout the reading, prompting me and nodding along. She shared her thoughts about the NDE world and the opportunity she had to speak at Findhorn, a large intentional community in Scotland, the following year. The reading resonated with her and she mentioned Gary Zukav's book, *The Dancing Wu Li Masters*, a mystical interpretation of quantum physics that had impressed her years earlier. She suggested that I read it.

As Barbara finished talking, I looked down at my recorder. It had shut off in the first few minutes of the reading—the result of electrical interference.

"The recorder shut off," I said as I stared at the machine. It seemed to turn off just as we were getting into the more intense parts of the reading.

"I warned you," she said.

So she had. Barbara and I signed off and promised to speak soon.

Electrical Sensitivity

Although you don't need to have an NDE to be electrically sensitive, electrical sensitivity is common among NDErs. That sensitivity is not limited to physical proximity. Barbara's reading was long distance, yet Barbara's energy invaded our space and altered it. Energy is not local, which is why readings can be performed at a distance, and it also explains why our energy continues to exist after our physical body dies, why the NDEr experiences events of the universe from hospital beds, on an operating table, or even underwater.

We will explore electrical sensitivity further in Chapter 13, when you will meet Mark Jacoby, "the man who talks to machines." We will look at our core energetic abilities, which appear to be enhanced through the NDE state.

I turned off my computer and glanced at my watch. Barbara and I had been talking for two hours. I began to reconstruct the interview and take notes.

An hour later, a walk sounded good. I walked down Montana Avenue, forcing myself to window shop. After the reading and the experience of going to another realm, I was glad to be out, surrounded by the bustle of crowds. Yet, I continued to think about the reading, about what I was learning about NDEs and what I hoped to learn.

The information I was shown went beyond the scope of Barbara's electrical sensitivity, an after-effect I was interested in. When Barbara mentioned she was electrically sensitive at the beginning of the reading, I was unsure what to do with that information. I had learned a lesson: A backup recorder and constant checking to see if the recording was working became necessary. Telling someone about their after-effects is one thing. Experiencing it for ourselves, as I had in Barbara's reading, shows how life must be adapted to take in these new powers.

Like Javier's reading, Barbara's reading was a clear message about consciousness—supported by experimental evidence. I would take that information and build on it in future readings. But first, I decided to take a deeper look into consciousness research. What was science saying about consciousness research, and what did I need to know about it? How did it fit with what I was learning about NDEs?

Mainstream Scientific Theories of Consciousness

I started by looking at the consensus theories on consciousness from mainstream science.

According to conventional science, most scientists believe the brain produces our conscious experience. This viewpoint is called the *materialist* perspective. Materialists believe reality is defined in terms of matter and that everything that exists is created by material objects. This materialist perspective does not acknowledge psi.

Yet, there is a new movement afoot—a movement that suggests consciousness needs to be interpreted from a broader reality, a reality coined *post-materialist science*.

According to post-materialism, additional information supports the concept that consciousness survives physical death and that the source of consciousness is non-material—which is what I was shown in Javier and Barbara's readings.

The scientists who support this view, Dr. Gary Schwartz, Dr. Mario Beauregard, Dr. Rupert Sheldrake, and others, state that science has failed to prove the brain is the creator of consciousness. These scientists also believe that individuals who experience physical death—near-death experiencers—may provide critical clues on the source and essence of consciousness. As I read this, I knew that my work reading for these experiencers was a step in the right direction, exploring an important link to the non-material world.

Material science might dismiss post-materialism as impossible. Yet, I was being told that consciousness is alive; it exists everywhere. And I was learning, independent of this viewpoint, that consciousness is indeed alive and a key factor in an NDE.

As I considered what was ahead for this work, I thought, *This process is like climbing a mountain blindfolded*. It would be nice to have something secure to hang on to, even if that might not be possible.

Because I'm a former researcher in the material world, I like facts. I like knowledge and affirmation. Yet I also understand that we cannot always know everything with certitude. This is especially true in the realm of the NDE. As unlikely as it may seem, my previous research experience was a good preparation for this new direction. In my previous work, nothing was ever known with 100-percent certainty. The pieces had to fit together; the patterns and trends had to be carefully analyzed, interpreted, and considered, to arrive at a conclusion. I considered this process as I thought about the puzzle of the NDE, consciousness, and the afterlife.

4 ❋ Lewis Brown Griggs and Physiological Transformation: ❋ Bodily Protection

"It is not you that is mortal, but only
your body. That man whom your
outward form reveals is not yourself;
the spirit is the true self."

—Cicero

My cell phone rang and I stepped outside the bistro in Westwood Village to answer it, clutching my tea. It was a number I didn't recognize—a California number. I tapped the green button and held the phone against my ear as young mothers pushing baby strollers streamed past.

The caller was the man who asked me to read for the experiencer at the IANDS (International Association for Near-Death Experiencers) conference in Crystal City—the man who first set me on my path to investigate near-death experiences. He promised he would contact me if he knew any other experiencers who would like to share their stories. In the meantime, I'd been making contact with more NDErs, meeting them, hearing about their journeys, and learning about their after-effects.

I took a seat on the bench on the tree-lined street as he asked how I liked the meeting, referring to the Orange County IANDS meeting several weeks earlier.

"Intriguing," I said, thinking back to the heady brew of interconnected worlds I'd encountered.

"It's a good little group," he said. "We've heard from so many over the years." He paused and his tone changed. "I've got another experiencer who wants to talk to you. She's expecting your call."

He then mentioned Jessica Haynes, who lives near Monterey, California. Jessica was interested in telling me about her NDE, which occurred after a near-fatal accident in Carmel. I thanked him and promised to call her. New people were being placed in front of me, and it was time to wade in more than waist-deep.

An Introduction to a Northern California NDEr With Extraordinary Properties

Jessica and I caught up via phone the following Thursday night.

While Jessica's experience happened more than 30 years ago, Jessica carries it with her every day, as real today as those many years ago. Today, Jessica is married to a commercial pilot, lives in Salinas, California, and is active in the NDE world through IANDS and her Website. When we chatted, I asked if she knew other experiencers who might want to share their stories.

"You need to speak to Lewis Brown Griggs," she said. "I saw him last weekend and I know he is interested." She gave me his number, but within minutes of hanging up, Lewis had emailed me and I read his story.

In March 1977, life as Lewis Brown Griggs knew it changed forever.

Lewis was driving his girlfriend's car in Berkeley, California, when a truck slid through a stop sign and crashed into the car. Lewis's head hit the windshield, and the car was totaled. On impact, Lewis realized he was dead. He left his body and entered a white tunnel. "It felt very peaceful," he said.

"There was total acceptance. My one regret was that I had no way of letting my family and girlfriend know that everything was okay. I was moving very fast into a tunnel of white light which radiated energy, love and peace.

"I would say it was 100% light and love. It was all around and permeating me. There were no boundaries, as if I had individuality and was merged with the light at the same time."

Then Lewis heard a voice, which he described as male and profound. He believed he was hearing the voice of God. "Lewis," the voice said. "You are called here to have this conversation and be sent back, because you are not doing your work."

"Okay," he said. "I surrender. Take me. I'm yours. I will do your work."

Lewis had always been a compliant individual who did what he was told. But he would find out that this was different.

"No, Lewis," the voice said. "It is not my work you have been called to do. It is your work."

"Well, what is my work?" Lewis asked.

Lewis had been struggling to find his way. His upbringing was of no help in discovering his true purpose, a life of meaning and depth.

"What is it, Lewis, that keeps you from being all that you are capable of being?"

At that point, Lewis was confused. His life seemed to be going along on its proscribed path even though he sometimes wondered if he was "supposed" to be doing something else. He didn't know what the voice meant. Was there something else Lewis was supposed to do?

"It must have something to do with the fact that I could never figure out how to bridge the gap between myself and anyone else from a different background," he thought.

"There it is Lewis," the Voice said. "That's your work."

Immediately, Lewis found himself whirling back down the tunnel into his body. "It was like putting on tight rubber gloves," he said. In an instant, he was back in his body. The ambulance had already arrived. "I was totally conscious in a totaled automobile with no physical damage," he said. Lewis walked up to the ambulance and asked, "What are you guys doing here?"

Transformation Following a Near-Fatal Crash

Despite the severe crash, Lewis was completely spared. Shortly after the accident, Lewis began to notice that his life was changing. He began to look at people in a new way, beyond the differences in culture, education, and wealth. Soon, Lewis decided to explore a new business that would embrace cross-cultural diversity as a path for corporations. Lewis became one of the first trainers in the field of diversity training—a field that would have been a stretch prior to his transformative experience.

"After my experience, I learned that what I am goes far beyond the ego, the mind, or body," Lewis said. "The essential core of all of us is the individual soul. My purpose now on earth is to let people know that we are all One and unique at the same time."

Like others, Lewis felt that after his experience, he had a mission. His purpose was to be more loving and kind, to be in service to others. His job was to distribute his knowing on a larger scale—in his case, to a world he understood. It was a sizable job, but in his small way, Lewis was meant to create another pillar of light on this earth.

Not all experiencers have so overt an experience and are given a direct mission. Some know they were given a mission, but can't remember it. Others don't recall being given one. Why was Lewis given this particular mission? Why Lewis?

Millions have admitted to experiencing an NDE. It's estimated that roughly 5 percent of the general population report near-death experiences according to the University of Liege in Belgium, but only a few are successful at living life at a higher power afterward. You can see that a lot has to break the right way for the experiencer to be successful. In Lewis's case, he eventually set up a plan and executed it. An ego-wall in his houseboat was decorated with articles about his company and his appearances on *Today* and *CBS Morning News*. Lewis had successfully unpacked his purpose.

Beyond his mission, Lewis's after-effect, bodily protection following a near-fatal accident, was intriguing, and I wanted to know more. After all, human tolerance for a crash of Lewis's type is poor. A collision of his type is usually fatal.

Jessica suggested I meet Lewis, who she described as a man from a world of wealth and privilege. Lewis was also interested in a reading and wanted to know more about his experience.

Jessica, Lewis, and I emailed back and forth for a few days and arranged to meet the day after Thanksgiving at Jessica's home in Salinas. Jessica was excited and decided to arrange a small party. The guest list included a top researcher who worked with Russell Targ in remote viewing, a nurse who worked with death and the dying, an author and lecturer, a radio show host, and a top psychic.

I celebrated Thanksgiving in the Hollywood Hills with my family in California. We munched on roasted pumpkin seeds, and the scent of the holiday—roasting turkey and cranberry sauce—filled the kitchen. I brought Hanukah presents for everyone. It was a quiet but loving evening and I left early, tired and satisfied.

I drove back to Santa Monica and went to sleep. Two hours later I woke up drenched in sweat.

I called Jessica the next morning. The trip was off. I could barely move. Lewis was already driving down from Sausalito to meet us but the meeting had to be postponed.

I felt terrible—disappointed. Then I got this message from Jessica:

Guess what? The same thing happened to me last night. Guests brought food to the party, and I got sick too. So I really feel for you. The party was great. Too bad we're both feeling poorly.

Jessica

We arranged to try again in two weeks. I would drive up and meet Lewis in Sausalito and catch up with Jessica on my way back to LA.

A Trip up the California Coast

Victorian houses overlook the waterfront in Sausalito. A collection of eclectic shops, yoga studios, and art galleries crowd the narrow streets. Lewis's houseboat is near town in Kappas Marina. We arranged to meet in the marina parking lot so we could walk together to his floating home.

I rounded the corner from town, pulled into a large lot, and was met by a tall man with thick white-blonde hair wearing a green windbreaker and waving his arms: Lewis. The foghorns from the harbor and the seagulls circling overhead signaled my arrival.

Like other NDErs, Lewis looks much younger than his 60+ years, as if he is ageless—frozen in time, a trait I noticed in all the NDErs.

As we walked along the dock to his home, Lewis tugging my suitcase, we chatted about my trip, Jessica, and his plans for my stay. We stopped in front of a charming houseboat with shutters and walked up several steps in the back to enter.

Lewis's houseboat with bleached wooden floors, throw rugs, and white overstuffed sofas was a scene from a Hollywood movie set. Except for looking outside and noting we were surrounded by water, we could have been in Beverly Hills. Lewis showed me to my bedroom, and I took in the queen-sized bed and the books on spirituality stacked on the oak nightstand. I tried not to think about lying down for a nap, as we had the reading and a local IANDS meeting to attend later that evening. Lewis had given me a warm welcome. This experience in California felt like I was in another country, a country that was accepting and warm.

"You'll hear the group leader talk about her NDE tonight, when she was a teaching assistant at Berkeley in the '60's," Lewis said as I returned downstairs and entered the living room. "Her experience was very different from mine."

"Have a seat," he said and gestured to the sofas in the living room. I sat on the wide sofa, and Lewis sat across from me and lit a candle. The fresh scent of pine filled the room.

Lewis stretched out his long legs and laced his fingers behind his head as he filled me in about his time at graduate school at Stanford. In another synchronicity, it turned out that others in his graduating class were individuals I knew from the investment business. We compared notes on the people we knew in common and chatted for a few minutes before we began our session.

I spread out a few crystals and explained how the reading would go. Lewis had had readings in the past and even told me how one psychic had predicted the end of his marriage. (She'd been right.) He couldn't wait to get going.

I mentioned, as I'd told others, that he could also ask questions in the reading. Lewis had many questions of his own about what happened and his life since then, so the reading would be a long one.

I told Lewis I was ready and we began.

Lewis's Session

As I settled in, Lewis reviewed his list and mine, and decided which questions he wanted to ask first. He was eager, and once the reading started, we uncovered a wealth of information.

I took a few deep breaths. I noticed a high-pitched noise and felt a wave of energy and warmth envelope me as I moved toward accessing higher vibrations. I was accustomed to the sound I heard in these readings because I was entering a higher vibrational space. It created an audible "buzz."

Reading for NDErs is unlike reading for any others. Whether they are young or old, male or female, professionals, students, or retirees, all the individuals I read for who are *not* NDErs have questions about their relationships, money, their families, health, and their careers. When I read for NDErs, it is a completely different experience. I enter a different realm. Time is simultaneous and vivid. I am there with the NDErs in their experience. With the NDErs, I step out into the universe. Lewis's reading would be no exception. I nodded that I was ready and Lewis asked the first question.

Lewis had seen the white light in his experience. "What was it?" he asked. He wondered if it played a role in his remarkable transformation.

Again, as we settled in, Spirit responded:

The light was Lewis's consciousness meeting universal consciousness. Imagine billions of individual consciousness united as one. Lewis's consciousness exited his body to connect with the total source where there is no top or bottom, no width or depth. That space is nothing and yet, it's everything. It's the stars and the universe, a deep well and the air we breathe. And when Lewis's consciousness encountered that space, he recognized it as a bright light, because there is no other way for source to convey it to us. No words exist in our vocabulary but the visual is the light.

I thought about this for a minute. The light is, of course, referred to throughout literature, religion, and spirituality and is closely related to the third eye in metaphysical work. In reality, it appears to be all souls, all beings, all sources, transposed into energy and united as one.

When experiencers see the white light, they might have different names for it, but many encounter it as they enter this other realm. It was their essence they took with them as they left their physical bodies behind. Some call it God; others recognize it as their soul families. Most describe it as all-encompassing love. Or the Universal All. It's there to greet us. It is what remains, the good, the true and pure, after we leave behind our earth bodies.

I looked up at Lewis out of the corner of my eye. He was sitting on the edge of the sofa, eager to continue. I heard a few seagulls squawking in the background and took another deep breath.

Lewis experienced a remarkable after-effect from his NDE. He was protected from a fatality. Not only did he experience this astonishing elixir after his crash, but it transformed Lewis in a way that no earthly experience, no material pursuits, ever could.

Lewis's experience in the tunnel and in his NDE enhanced his purpose and remedied his cultural bias. He returned reformed and remodeled. I mouthed the words coming from Spirit:

As our soul begins to separate from the body, its intent is much more metaphysically focused. Rather than focusing on earthly pursuits, it begins to search for true meaning. Which it finds immediately in this other realm.

An Experiencer's Background

I wanted to know about Lewis's past. Not about how he was the descendant of two governors and founders of major U.S. corporations, nor how he attended an Ivy League School, worked in Republican politics, and had a job in public television. I wanted to know about his life as a young child. What really happened to Lewis when he was growing up? I asked if there was anything in his background or upbringing that was linked to his NDE? I turned all my awareness to what was happening inside me as I focused. I had to see if I could find an answer that made sense to this issue of upbringing, because the door had already been opened in Barbara's reading (see Chapter 3).

Spirit responded.

Lewis was like a god growing up. An idol to his family, loved for his lineage, his outer qualities, his good looks. He grew up out of touch with his power. Despite his grace, his education, and background, he foundered. Those attributes weren't the answer for Lewis.

I learned a great deal from Spirit about Lewis that day. Like other NDErs, Lewis scanned the road signs along the way as he tried to establish his identity as an individual. Like others, prior to his NDE Lewis went through emotional trauma as he tried to make his way in a world in which he questioned his role. His quest wasn't getting any easier; it was getting worse. He found himself at a crossroads, between an inflection point and being just plain stuck. He repeatedly came back empty-handed attempting to define himself beyond his legacy. Personal issues were left unresolved.

A pattern emerged and issues multiplied, from his childhood into his adulthood. Life got stickier as Lewis grew older.

But Spirit is always evaluating that vulnerability. For individuals like Lewis, consciousness is susceptible and ready to be triggered. This trigger does not appear to be a totally random event. There is no coincidence that these people have reached an impasse, and under the right set of circumstances, an NDE results. These individuals spend more time contemplating the universe and are less attached to their physical bodies. An out-of-body experience seems more natural to them and may be a part of their progression as they search for something true and real and good. And the universe appears to play a part, determining the right moment.

Was Lewis chosen for his experience? Was he on a radar screen to identify emotionally vulnerable people for a new, renewed purpose? Like others, it's almost as if Lewis was evaluated and the results—the seeking, the vulnerability, the timing—were enough to select him.

Lewis emerged from his totaled car unscathed. Did some invisible force protect him as he left his body? How did Lewis dodge trauma? How did he walk away from a totaled vehicle? These were the questions we posed next.

Lewis, and all of us, are much more than our physical bodies. Lewis's physical body and the accident were merely the conduits to facilitate his transformation. Once Lewis accepted his mission, and was infused and altered by the light, the physical negativity of the accident was absolved. Lewis was made whole.

Is higher consciousness a cure for earthly issues? New agers, mystics, and the world's religions have claimed this all along. Getting in touch with our higher selves can improve our health and our overall state of being, many claim. The nature of an NDE even appears to be a cure for fatal trauma. Should we regard higher consciousness as the gift of completeness?

The topic of the therapeutic possibilities of mystical experiences is still in its infancy, yet it appears to be correlated with the beneficial after-effects of near-death experiences. Clinical trials at several universities, including NYU, are underway and show that "individuals transcend their primary identification with their bodies and experience ego-free states... and return with a new perspective and profound acceptance," according to one researcher.[1] Cases from this NDE research even suggest that the effects of NDEs go beyond this to include healing.

Lewis's accident miraculously not only resolved his personal issues but also provided him with superhuman protection. What occurred during his NDE to transform Lewis? Was it a mysterious transference from the universe? Or was he just plain lucky?

NDEs have the propensity to heal. The spiritual literature is replete with stories of spontaneous healing, and in Chapter 5 you will meet another NDEr, Rajiv Parti, who experienced remarkable healing from his NDE. Does consciousness have the ability to override physical reality? And if so, what are its implications for modern medicine?

Lewis's Higher Authority

Why was Lewis's higher authority not only God but a white, male God? Why wasn't Lewis given Buddha? Or his grandfather? Why a white, male God?

Spirit responded: *NDEs are administered by an authority figure in the experiencer's vernacular. One they can recognize and respect. For an elite, white male, who would that authority figure be but an Episcopal, white, male God? Someone of Lewis's world. A trigger in Lewis's consciousness appears to be linked to the right source, just as it is for every NDEr. Lewis was instructed by a voice he could understand and respect so he would pay close attention. It had to be a voice that would be credible and make an impression on him. After all, this was a teaching experience.*

I stopped and looked up. "How are we doing for time?" I asked as I took a breath.

"We're good," Lewis said glancing at his watch. "Keep going."

When Lewis returned to his body, it occurred with a painful snap, almost a trauma, like Barbara had experienced. Why would it be painful for our consciousness, an element lighter than air, to re-enter our bodies? Why not smoothly? After all, consciousness is feather-light.

"How is consciousness supposed to get back into the body?" I wondered as I waited for Spirit to deliver the answer.

When our consciousness reenters our body, it happens with a lurch. This event is not meant to take place on earth. When it occurs as part of an NDE, it's like an operation that hasn't been perfected. We exist on earth as a complete, unified package—physical body and consciousness interwoven. They are not meant to be separated. We are born with the two intertwined but if consciousness is separate for too long at a higher plane, getting them back together is unwieldy and difficult.

Lewis looked at his watch: five o'clock. We would have to finish the reading. Lewis asked a few more questions about his life and his work, and then it was time to end our session and get ready for the local IANDS meeting.

It took several seconds for my eyes to focus. The sun had gone down and the room was lit by the glow of candles. Lewis turned the lights back on. We sat for a minute in silence.

Lewis's Experience and My Thoughts on NDErs

I thought about what I had been shown in Lewis's reading. It seemed as if each NDE was customized to suit the individual's personality, beliefs, and culture. Yet, there was a universality to the experience—this was an experience about all of us. About life. Hope. Spirit. Death. All of that.

Where was this all leading? For me, I could see I was moving toward a viewpoint that verged on the border of science and spirituality—an idea that we are all participating in the same energy. That everything that was happening had a spiritual message to teach us, a message that underlies our lives. I learned that we may not readily recognize the source or the message, but it was there, even if it was hidden below the surface. The work showed me that synchronicities weren't really coincidences, but something more intentional. That the universe, and its impact, is much larger than we perceive. That our connectedness is pervasive.

I thought about the experiencer who served as the conduit for this journey—the man with the artistic after-effects. He had been given an immense talent. A gift. Yet, he had difficulty proceeding with his mission—difficulty accepting it. Others I met had agreed to accept their missions. Each one was sent back to do his or her work. Some succeeded. Others fell by the wayside. All of this also seemed to be part of a grander scheme.

5 ✴ Ragiv Parti and Physiological Transformation: ✴ Spontaneous Healing

> "What drains your spirit drains your body.
> What fuels your spirit fuels your body."
> —Caroline Myss

California was a gold mine. Everyone wanted to talk about their NDEs—even if they never had one.

I continued to speak with experiencers, and one morning, as I clicked through emails under the green Starbucks umbrella on Montana Avenue, an email from a childhood experiencer popped up. This man's IQ had risen 20 points since his NDE. I clicked on the next email, this one from a Disney artist, also a childhood experiencer. Because there was no way to measure the after-effects for childhood experiencers, I filed these cases away. I paged through more emails, including one from a woman who had become very spiritual since her NDE. There were emails from several experiencers who became psychic. I set those aside, too.

I scanned an email from a man with poetry as an after-effect, and another from a woman with spontaneous healing. I studied a note from a lawyer whose mental processes sped up. I spoke to a woman who took up the flute, and another who improvised music. I made notes of all of their experiences.

I put together a Website and experiencers got the word out. Soon the news spread. Many were very eager to speak about their NDEs. One such person was Dr. Rajiv Parti.

As I sat outside the coffee shop on Montana Avenue, the sky translucent blue in every direction, I thought about how I would miss this weather—80-degree days, not a cloud in the sky—when I returned to the East Coast.

The phone rang. It was Dr. Parti. I set down my iced tea and listened to his story. I had a million questions, but I waited as he filled me in.

Dr. Parti's NDE

Dr. Parti's experience occurred on Christmas Day in 2010.

Dr. Parti's typical day, as chief of cardiac anesthesiology at Bakersfield Heart Hospital, usually began at 6 a.m. He would be rushing to work, talking to a nurse or his stock broker. He might be driving his sports Mercedes or his BMW. Maybe his Hummer. If someone cut him off on the road, he'd go after them.

Every two or three years, Dr. Parti and his family would move. Eventually his house was so big that Dr. Parti and his wife needed iPhones to find the kids. His mortgage was $15,000 per month.

One day, he received a call from his doctor. "I have good news and bad news," he said. All Dr. Parti heard was the bad news: prostate cancer. Dr. Parti flew to Florida for surgery. The surgery went fine, but soon he became incontinent and experienced pelvic pain. After seven more surgeries, one of which led to abdominal infections, Dr. Parti became depressed and was placed on three anti-depressants. After three years, his infection worsened and he became addicted to pain pills.

Finally, in 2010, a UCLA physician made the decision to perform another surgery.

Dr. Parti was in excruciating pain with a 105-degree fever when he was ambulanced to UCLA Medical Center. His infection had spread to his blood and sepsis was setting in.

While he was on the operating table, Dr. Parti experienced his NDE.

Dr. Parti's Session

I arranged to meet with Dr. Parti in Los Angeles a week after our conversation. His daughter attended USC, like my son, and Dr. Parti was in town frequently, so we would meet in person very soon.

At 2:00 p.m. the following Thursday, I heard a knock on my door. Dr. Parti was dressed casually in an open-neck shirt and khakis, a doctor on his day off. I waved him inside. We chatted as he walked over to the small glass and metal table and the two chairs I had set up in the middle of the room for our session.

Dr. Parti emailed me multiple times prior to our meeting. When we finally met, he had already filled out the questionnaire and we had spoken on the phone. I had made notes about his Website and the talks he had given. I had a long list of questions based on our conversation, his answers to the questionnaire, his talks, and his Website, and I was eager to explore his experience.

We began the session. I closed my eyes to ground myself. As the session opened, I felt Spirit's presence and found myself at the beginning of Dr. Parti's NDE.

Dr. Parti's NDE began in a constricting way, as if he couldn't breathe—as if his soul was traveling and trying to break through to the next realm. I told Dr. Parti that I saw his father and experienced a sense of dread when I saw him.

Dr. Parti's forehead creased in thought. "I was afraid of my father. He used to beat me," he said. As a child, Dr. Parti was once beaten so severely he couldn't return to school for three weeks.

Dr. Parti experienced his life review with his father, the primary authority figure in his life, even though his father had passed away 20 years earlier. Dr. Parti's father was the individual Dr. Parti most respected, whom he would listen to.

Following his life review, Dr. Parti forgave his father for his abuse and together, father and son, hand in hand, entered a tunnel.

The reading continued.

Dr. Parti encountered a white light, meant to cleanse and purify him—to start him on his new journey through the darkness.

On the other side of the tunnel, Dr. Parti was greeted by two entities who said they were the angels of strength and healing, symbols of significance for a man of healing. When his wife later asked him, "What happened to the thousands of Indian gods and goddesses?" Dr. Parti had no answer for her.

The session continued with a particular rhythm. The soundtrack of the readings was a constant low, back-and-forth buzz of communication that I listened to and presented. I was the medium, meant to convey the information, the interchange between two worlds of information that filtered through me.

During his NDE, Dr. Parti encountered past lives. He floated over a meadow filled with roses and a clear mountain stream. He saw colors, fractured like a kaleidoscope. "I could hear a distant chime which sounded like 'om,'" he said. Peace. The holiest mantra there is and the symbol of the primal frequency of existence.

Dr. Parti's experience was like a kaleidoscope of infinite possibilities, occurring simultaneously. From the meadow, the light spoke to Dr. Parti, and he was told that he was not good to his patients. Dr. Parti was given the realization that he was going back. That he would lead a more spiritual life and fulfill his soul contract.

Dr. Parti experienced another unusual occurrence during his NDE: A veridical experience—one that was verified by others upon his return.

While Dr. Parti lay on the operating table, he remembers hearing the anesthesiologist's jokes. He felt his consciousness travel to India, where he saw his sister, wearing blue jeans and a red shirt, and his mother, wearing a green sari, having tea. When he spoke to his mother two days later, she confirmed that the two of them were having tea, dressed in that clothing, at the time of his NDE.

When Dr. Parti woke up from his surgery, he explained to his doctors that he could hear their jokes during his procedure. They replied that he must have been light on anesthesia.

But was there another explanation? Did Dr. Parti's consciousness exist in all space and time? Did his higher mind simply visit his mother and sister as part of his experience?

Dr. Parti's Transformation

Within 72 hours of his NDE, Dr. Parti's fever was down. His addiction to pain medicine was gone, his depression healed, and his chronic pain evaporated. He was cured of prostate cancer and sepsis.

Did Dr. Parti experience a miracle? Or was there a simpler explanation?

Within three weeks of his NDE, Dr. Parti changed his life style. He resigned from his job and became a vegetarian. He sold his high-end cars and bought a hybrid. A plastic surgeon bought his house, and Dr. Parti and his family moved into a house half the size. He began meditating instead of drinking to relax.

Following his NDE, Dr. Parti shed everything about himself that had been touched by his former life. He could no longer be bound by earthly events once he experienced his spiritually transformative experience.

Today, Dr. Parti has his feet in two worlds: the earth and the universe. Like most NDErs, he's walking a tightrope, and there's a tension in that space he inhabits. It's as if Dr. Parti is two people now, and it's a struggle every day for him to manage these two. He has difficulties trying to fit into the earth plane after experiencing complete perfection and total love in the universe.

For NDErs, the day-to-day is a struggle on a journey without a compass. Falling off the path temporarily seems to also be a part of the process. Dr. Parti is still adapting to his new world, this world he was deposited in after his NDE.

When we asked in his session if Dr. Parti was a candidate for his experience, this is what we were told:

Like others, Dr. Parti possessed particular qualities. The ability to be awakened yet a sufficient amount of darkness. He could be transformed into a living light after his experience, if he was capable of serving.

I glanced up at Dr. Parti. He was leaning forward, listening intently.

"Are you okay?" I asked.

He nodded. "What happened that caused my transformation?" Dr. Parti asked.

Dr. Parti's physiological after-effects included spontaneous healing from a fatal disease as well as addiction and depression. This is no small feat. According to what we know of science, being cured of cancer, a fatal disease, along with addiction and sepsis where the risk of death is high, is not just remarkable but inexplicable.

Spirit clarified: *The higher vibration Dr. Parti experienced in his NDE appeared to wipe out earth-bound maladies. The afflictions of the physical body simply do not exist on a higher plane of pure, high frequency energy. Like Lewis, Dr. Parti is more than his physical body.*

In Dr. Parti's case, a shift was accomplished at a soul level. The non-physical state. The healing that accompanied this shift created a powerful charge and Dr. Parti was literally surrounded by the light. The light has the ability to transform, including physical healing, due to its highly energetic properties.

During Dr. Parti's NDE, he encountered a peaceful energy that was all-empowering—so absolute that he felt, almost for the first time in his life, that he was complete. Dr. Parti tried to bring back that heightened state with him to earth. Like other NDErs, he longed for that elevated time, to immerse himself in that realm. That elevated state didn't last though, and he returned to his body with a thud. It was a shock for Dr. Parti to find that our world is static, yet he set off with determination to find that state again. And even though he had traveled to that distant realm once, he couldn't achieve it again. It was simply not available to him on earth.

This is important information, because NDErs, like us everyday folk, are interested in achieving the higher state of the NDE when they return to earth, but are unable to do so.

You can't really come back from an NDE. You return because your body returns. But you—the essence of you—doesn't really come back. Your essence is transformed forever. It's merged with the universe. Nothing is familiar yet you're supposed to carry on as if you had not been altered.

Communication From Beyond

During our session, I asked who was I talking to and was told the following:

You don't know us but you know us and will meet us. Encounter us. We are here to do good deeds and we are all around you. You can never see us. We are beautiful people but not people. Beautiful beings. What you people call beings.

This was too much to comprehend as it came to me. I needed to stop. I took a drink of water and paused, then nodded to Dr. Parti that I could continue.

"What do I need to know?" I asked. I figured if "they" were going to answer, I should ask another question.

You're asking too many questions, they said. *You just need to accept. The people who accept have mastered this. They have successfully incorporated this and can go forth. Many can't put the pieces together. They have to be left by the wayside but it's part of the process.*

This reading was different because Spirit communicated directly to me, telling me that acceptance is key to understanding—advice for me, but also for all of us. I was told that my earthbound way of going about things, seeking answers, may not be the way to go.

I looked up and shifted in my seat. I had to go forward with the reading so we continued. I asked Dr. Parti about the background of his NDE next.

There were moments of joy and happiness in his experience, but there were also many intense moments. Why did Dr. Parti experience extremes of joy and darkness in his NDE? Did he need to be shown something else—something more extreme—to get him off his current path?

What Dr. Parti was shown was done to shape and mold his conscious-ness so that he could move forward and expand, to touch more and more people on his journey when he returned.

Then we asked: What was Dr. Parti meant to learn from his experience?

That there is peace, tranquility, comfort, and everlasting contentment available to him. Dr. Parti was meant to know this but more importantly, it was meant to seep into him.

Prior to his experience, Dr. Parti had never been interested in any-thing spiritual. Now, all had changed. What was the trigger? Was the uni-verse watching? Did they say, *This guy needs to be shown something of a higher purpose?* Because it worked. Like other NDErs, Dr. Parti now car-ries the message of transformation within him forever.

When Dr. Parti returned, he was no longer interested in his former career and began to search for meaning in his life. The NDE had sent him off on a journey.

Their Experience/My Experience

Dr. Parti's experience was real. I was there with him, and it was vivid and intense. I have touched it and tasted it. I saw what he saw and felt what he felt—just as I saw and experienced Javier's NDE, as well as Barbara and Lewis's. My experiences in these sessions were the same as the NDErs', and trying to describe this realm and its mysteries was as difficult for me as for them. As William James, noted Harvard psychologist and profes-sor, said when he first defined noetic experiences back in 1902, there is an "ineffability" to them, the inability to express or describe them in words.

Spontaneous Healing: A Rare but Real Phenomenon

How did Dr. Parti's healing occur? How did his maladies disappear? As if he had never suffered addiction. Never been depressed. Never had cancer.

Think of the after-effects of an NDE like re-booting your computer. Except when you reboot from an NDE, you're life is no longer version 2.0. Now it's version 20.0. You and your life have been transformed from a cosmic reboot. It's a simple concept on the face of it, but let's pick it apart and examine its true meaning.

Picture this for yourself. You have the same outer warehouse as when you left your physical body. But the inner components have been boosted—rewired. With new operating instructions from Source, and a dose of pure unfiltered energy unlike any we are able to obtain on earth. Without our physical bodies, this energy's potency is enhanced. It's pure essence. Pure light. Pure consciousness. It returns with us to earth, enhancing us through a process that's been updated by the universe.

This additional essence is the gift of the NDE—what we are meant to make use of as we set off on our new journey. On earth, our physical body creates imbalances and illness—both physical and emotional—stress and suffering. When experiencers return from their NDE, they possess a dose of powerful energy that not only raises the body's vibration, but is capable of wiping out maladies. In Dr. Parti's case, this powerful energy brushed up against his physical body and caused a healing that shifted his essence.

Dr. Parti soaked up this perfect, total energy as it was discharged into him. Dr. Parti was no longer just his physical body. He was more than his physical body when this infusion produced an override of existing corruptions.

When you reboot your computer, you go for a clean slate. Like a hard reboot, a near-death experience is an extreme solution to reset the system. The near-death experience sweeps away faults and wipes away corruptions. Like a reboot, it's the last resort.

Since his NDE, Dr. Parti has been switched on. He is literally a new man. He has shed everything that was touched by the earth and been stripped down to his elemental, metaphysical core. The shift that he experienced was completed at a soul level.

It's not easy to understand all of this. We can only try to process as much as we are shown.

Once you go to this other plane, you're forever transformed. You come back to earth because your body comes back. But "you"—the essence of you—doesn't really come back. It's altered forever and it's almost impossible to reconcile.

When the session was over, I asked Dr. Parti about his family. How were they adjusting to his new life?

His wife and daughter are supportive, he said, but the reaction of others has been mixed. I sensed that he was feeling his way, a path different from his days as a high-powered physician. As time has passed, I've noticed pictures on his Facebook page, pictures of his wife and daughter, and a lovely letter to his wife on their anniversary, thanking her for her part in his journey. His journey—and the journey of his family—will continue.

Dr. Parti and I shook hands and he left. His had been an intense reading—and different. When I read for NDErs, I am the channel, not the experiencer. My job is to transmit the information and analyze how it fits with what I already know and am still learning. But my emotional response is distinct from the NDErs'.

In this reading with Dr. Parti, something peculiar happened. "They" had communicated directly with me, telling me to approach this work differently. To stop using earth tactics. To accept. I thought about it. It made sense yet it was a challenge for me to try to accept it. I kept going anyway. I'm only human.

As I closed the front door and reentered the apartment, a question came to me: What is the connective tissue between all of these experiences? What was it that I was being shown, that would link these experiencers together? I hadn't identified it but knew that the link was there.

We think we can look at the evidence and find the answers but sometimes the more we examine, the more questions arise. Yet some force told me: *The answers are out there. Keep going.*

Moving Back East

I rambled around the apartment packing up for my move in two days. My stay in California had come to an end. My classes were winding up, my short-term lease was expiring, and it was time to return home. The welcome had been warm and Californians had been supportive of the work. And I'd been in California to pursue this work; I knew that now.

I had connected with many experiencers, hospice nurses, academics, physicists, service workers, and therapists. Yet, in spite of the support, I was still very much on my own. I, too, was traveling my own unique journey, much like the NDErs. *This is who I am*, I thought as I looked around the room at the last few items I would ship home.

I felt comfortable in California, where the approach to the metaphysical world was matter-of-fact. Walking down the street in the bright, warm weather, I thought about how I would miss Southern California. But at the same time, my family, my friends and my connections were back east. The opportunity to immerse myself in another place had been a short gift, but it was time to resume my former life.

The room suddenly felt swelteringly hot. I opened a window and breathed deeply as the light in the room dimmed.

6 ✳ Dan Rhema and Dr. Robert Magrisso and Cognitive Transformation: ✳ Artistic Ability

> "To send light into the darkness of men's
> hearts—such is the duty of the artist."
>
> —Robert Schumann

Back in Baltimore, I headed down North Avenue to the Maryland Institute College of Art, past row houses and check-cashing outlets, and thought about Diane Willis. Diane, an experiencer herself, runs the Chicago IANDS (International Association for Near-Death Experiencers) group, an active near-death chapter. She had mentioned to me that Bob Magrisso, an internist in Evanston, Illinois, experienced an NDE and returned with artistic gifts. She suggested I contact him.

When I called Bob, I wasn't surprised to learn that he and I were connected in other ways. (Each NDEr seemed to share a link with me, I learned as time went on.) For one, he had spent time in Baltimore while attending Johns Hopkins University.

Robert Magrisso: A Scientist Influenced by the Afterlife

Bob Magrisso teaches at Northwestern University Medical School, trained at Albert Einstein College of Medicine, and earned a master's degree in biomedical engineering from Johns Hopkins University. Bob's undergraduate degree is in physics. He is now a practicing internist in Evanston, Illinois. When Bob and I spoke that first time, he told me about his experience. When he was 48, he experienced a massive coronary and lay unconscious in the Evanston Hospital emergency room as his medical colleagues worked to save his life:

"Seconds prior to the arrest, I heard a sound like loud crickets. I recall being in another world, like a star-filled night sky. I felt extreme peace and freedom. There was a movement toward three lights—which I later imagined as beings. I had the feeling of pure consciousness. There was no sense of wanting anything," Bob said.

When Bob regained consciousness, the emergency room physician in charge of the resuscitation had tears in his eyes. "We got you back!" he said. "Did you see the white light?"

"No, but I was going up the black tunnel," Bob said.

Bob told me, "I am not sure where those words came from but they described the feeling of movement toward the three lights. I quickly determined these were my father, who had died in August 1993, my best friend Tomas, who died in August 1991, and a more distant friend, Raphael who had died only a week before this experience. I don't know how I 'knew' it was them, but I did. I felt they were there to welcome me."

Bob described his experience as "a sense of 'awakening' from what I knew. Maybe the most positive feelings I have ever had."

Bob and I made plans to Skype the following week. On the following Wednesday evening, I checked the time: 30 minutes until I would call Bob.

At 8:00 p.m., I dragged my chair closer to the computer and peered through the screen at a pleasant, round-faced man with curly gray hair. I turned on the recorder; I checked the recorder periodically to make sure that we didn't lose our connection.

I had a few questions for Bob about his experience and his background. I was also particularly curious about Bob's return to his body. How was that decision made? I decided to simply ask him.

"I did not make that decision," he said. "It just happened. I did not want to die. I felt like my life was a complete failure before this event. I felt so sad that I would not see my wife and family again."

That sense of failure was a theme that would come up with experiencers I spoke to. Even individuals as accomplished as Bob felt as if they had not lived their lives completely. Many expressed profound sorrow at never having the opportunity to see their loved ones again, too, if they did not return from their NDEs.

Both Bob and I wanted to investigate his after-effects. Bob, a physician and scientist, returned from his near-death experience with the need to produce art. His paintings and mixed media works repeatedly portray stars and mystical symbols as metaphors. Like others you will meet in *Life After Near Death*, there is an unceasing, repetitive, compulsive aspect to Bob's activity after his NDE. Bob dabbled in art prior to his experience, but spiritual figures began to appear in Bob's work after his NDE: ladders reaching to the universe. Planets. Beings floating in space.

"I often use the star-filled night sky as a background because it puts everything in perspective," he says. Bob's work includes three-dimensional pieces, collages, and wood carvings. The language of his art is highly symbolic, more so since his NDE.

Like other NDErs, Bob says his experience taught him there is more to our physical reality than we know or understand. His art strives to express the mystery at the heart of reality, and he uses his work to investigate his own spirituality as well. According to a review at a college that recently exhibited his work, "Magrisso's work suggests a journey into the deeper human spirituality seeking enlightenment."

Bob agrees with the assessment that his post-NDE art reflects a deeper spirituality, a greater meaning and purpose. "It's hard for me to fake that," he adds. "I feel like doing the art is a way of getting a little closer to that same experience. Through the art, I am able to somehow bridge that experience. Like I'm trying to get back to some kind of awareness of the universe."

In his collage work, Bob sometimes uses the mandala, a traditional pattern, as a symbolic representation of the cosmos. It's his way to tie together the present and the ancient in his artistic language. Other NDErs also employ universal symbols from their NDEs (as you will see when you meet Lynnclaire Dennis in Chapter 11).

"The less I think about what is there, the better," Bob says. "Death, grief, healing, and wholeness are some of the themes I gravitate toward—themes I encounter daily in my professional life." These are also themes that arise after near-death experiences. And the aspect of not exploring it consciously but allowing it to arise from the sub-conscious is a theme I would hear over and over again from other experiencers who had made peace with their new behavior.

Bob's Session

I took three deep breaths and felt myself sink into my body as I prepared to seek the answers to the sounds Bob heard, the images he saw, the meaning of his artwork.

It was difficult to ground Bob. Like other NDErs, Bob was not tethered—I suspected from his overload of consciousness. As I began to read Bob's energy, I noted that his aura was light-filled and, like others, he appeared to have two distinct auras. One aura was completely white and filmy, and encased his body. The other aura, dark and muddy, showed physical trauma from his heart attack. Having two auras was becoming a distinct sign of an NDE.

We asked, "What did Bob receive in his NDE that influenced his artwork?"

Spirit showed me how Bob's mental unfoldment was heightened in his NDE. His experience produced a permanently accessible higher mind, which Bob uses to convey imagery to the public, through his use of symbols and signs. Sometimes symbols are all we have to communicate, I was learning. The language of this other plane was illusive and didn't conform to our known signatures for life.

The sound he heard—the crickets. What was that? (Other NDErs also comment on hearing sounds as they leave their bodies. It's one of the 16 classical elements of an NDE. See Appendix A.)

That sound is the vibration of a rising frequency, which is encountered as our consciousness whirls out of our physical body to ascend the physical plane. We interpret this as "sound" although it may be another property.

I looked up. I heard a siren, a police car passing down the street. I waited for the noise to subside, then lowered my head and continued.

"The stars Bob experienced, which repeat as images in his artwork, are recurrent themes in NDE art. What do the stars mean in Bob's work?" Bob and I wondered. Stars are repeated as metaphors throughout NDEs and all of the individuals I spoke to asked about their meaning. Why are NDErs shown stars? Why not the moon? Or sun?

Bob's stars are long lasting impressions of the universe he traveled to, the universe he is permanently connected to. Parts of Bob belong to that realm and were birthed there. As Bob traveled through the black tunnel, he left the dense, oppressive space where trauma lives to enter a vast, star-filled realm of infinite light, a beautiful and peaceful space.

"Bob identified the lights as his friends. Was he correct?" we asked. I glanced up at Bob and he nodded back to continue.

The lights were the essence of his friends, there to meet him, just as others have been greeted by the light, personal or collective friends and family, Spirit said. This answer was in keeping with Bob's understanding and my newfound understanding of the light.

The light can also be interpreted as the universe's response to our earth's darkness. In fact, one of Bob's works, "Lightbearers," is an assemblage of images of more than 30 individuals who Bob consider bearers of "light."

"I see them as not only human, but also bringers of light to the collective darkness in which we dwell," says Bob.

Bob's Mission

Bob was also interested in his mission after his NDE. Mission was one of Bob's main questions and, as others did, Bob expressed his question in his reading in terms of "mission"—not life purpose, or job, or life path. He and others conveyed a sense of assignment.

"What more specifically is the mission I should be fulfilling?" Bob asked. Although Bob is producing art and serving his community, he wonders if he should be doing more.

Your job is to continue to access, download, and transmit a higher consciousness you received, through your healing and your artwork. When people stand in front of your art, it seeps into them, it registers unconsciously. Your elevated consciousness is transmitted through your work. Your job is to continue to access the light, download and transmit it.

"Does that make sense?" I asked Bob.

"Yes."

"Do you think you do that?" I asked.

"I try. I think that happens. I don't know if I mentioned it to you but I've been involved in a spiritual path for 40 years. (Bob is now 68.) And that is part of the intention in all the things I do," he said.

And there it was: the intent that Bob had before his experience. He was a seeker prior to his NDE. Searching for the other. On a very intentional path.

How Did Bob Arrive at His NDE?

Like others, Bob had been moving in the direction of his NDE for years. The NDE was just the last step. Or maybe it was the first step? In his case, it seemed very intentional. He was seeking something, asking for it prior to his NDE. He got it.

"What did Bob's life look like prior to his NDE?" I wondered. He mentioned he had been in a spiritual practice for years, but what about the rest of Bob's life, beyond his spiritual pursuits? Bob and I explored this in our next question.

Prior to his NDE, Bob's life had a pattern. He was drowning in the same routine but not progressing beyond his boundaries—boundaries established by convention and others. But these conventions didn't particularly suit him.

We were told that Bob was not really growing. He kept experiencing the same things over and over. It was routine and it was limiting—and it wasn't enough. In a sense, he was spinning his wheels. "I was in somewhat of a crisis about the spiritual path," he said. "In fact, I sometimes would joke that I was having a mid-life crisis. This sort of solved it. Really."

Here's what Spirit had to say:

Bob was raised with certain expectations for what he would achieve and how he would fulfill his obligations. He did what was expected of him, even though part of him rebelled. He fulfilled those expectations anyway and at the age of 48, he had a crisis. Or perhaps the crisis started earlier? Bob found himself in a box and the box kept getting smaller and smaller, until the NDE freed him from that box.

This was similar to Lewis's life prior to his NDE (see Chapter 4): expectations that must be fulfilled even while the soul yearned for something more.

"Did some force look at Bob's situation and say, 'He's ready now'?" I wondered.

There is a point, when people in situations similar to Bob, with emotional trauma in their past yet the capability for so much more, yearn for an alternative. But they don't know how to get there. Or they can't get there. At a certain point, an inflection point, they are pulled out of their bodies to be re-awakened. They return to carry on, but in a new way, a different way. On a different path.

Bob agreed. "It was really, like you say, that spinning your wheels kind of thing." Overall, Bob says that his experience left him "with the sense that I—all of us—are a part of something bigger," a sentiment shared by other NDErs.

Dan Rhema: A CEO Transformed to a Shamanic Artist

Let's look at Dan Rhema, another experiencer who returned with art as an NDE after-effect. Was Dan's transformation similar to Bob's?

The following Wednesday, shortly after 6:00 a.m., I opened my eyes to the sound of a low buzzing. It took me a second to realize the sound was my iPhone alarm. Today I would read for Dan, a former not-for-profit CEO who had been transformed to a Shamanic artist.

I made my way to the kitchen, fixed a cup of tea, and took the tea out to my patio. The sun was just coming up on the skyline. I could see the top of the elms beyond the apartments to the west. My thoughts drifted to how this work was unfolding and how I first contacted Dan.

Being in California and doing this work had been easy. It was accepted on the West Coast, and many experiencers came forward to share their stories. But once I was back on the East Coast, things were different. Not everyone viewed this work the same way in the more traditional Mid-Atlantic. That aside, I knew that my ability—the coincidences—and my desire, were pointing me in the right direction, the direction of progressing down this path. There was a reason I was doing this work and meeting the specific people who had come into my life. I also knew my ability to read for them wasn't a coincidence. I considered my background in research. None of this was a coincidence; I was convinced. As I sat on my patio, I pulled out a crystal from my pocket and looked at it. "Go forward," it seemed to say.

I met Dan indirectly. I first heard him talk about his NDE on a radio show. I checked his Website and noted that one of the tabs is labeled "When I Was a Ghost." Intrigued, I contacted him, and he responded quickly. I thought back to my conversation with Dan as I sipped my tea and waved to my neighbor, who had stepped out for his newspaper and disappeared, leaving me to my thoughts once again.

Dan's NDE was brought on by a bout with dengue fever, meningitis, and encephalitis in 1991. When his wife, Susan, asked the doctors what his prognosis was, they said, "We don't know. We can't find any literature on anyone who has survived this."

Dan survived and went on to become an artist, a 180-degree reversal from his former profession as president of an international training center in Mexico.

As his illness worsened, Dan was flown to the CDC Hospital in Atlanta and admitted. When they gave Dan a spinal, he shot out of his body and was thrown up to the corner of the room. He floated away in complete blackness to an unexpected journey to the other side. During Dan's NDE, he ended up in the time of pre-religion. Cave dwellers.

"I believe I was thrown into that part of subconscious that was pre-history. Early. Shamanic," he says. "I don't have the desire to follow any kind of religion now. I feel like I went somewhere else. Beyond that. Or before that."

During his NDE, Dan heard a voice. "You understand you're dying now?" the voice said.

At that point, Dan felt he was being given a choice between dying and coming back. His wife and daughters were still across the border. Dan understood he could die, but also knew that his wife and daughters were not there. He made a choice. Dan returned.

Inspired by the Universe

But, as I'm sure you can anticipate, Dan did not return as the same person. Within a couple months, he began to have intense visions at night. As soon as Dan goes to sleep, he's overtaken by a heightened consciousness that feeds him otherworldly images: burning stars, third eyes, Shamanic faces.

This was the beginning of Dan's visionary art process. Today, Dan's days are spent moving back and forth between a dream space and consciousness. His cycles of image downloads last up to six months and completely take over his life, until he's completely spent in a cycle of art production. Dan has been making art compulsively for the last 15 years.

Dan doesn't make art the way a traditional artist would. He paints with his fingers and a rag. His colors are intense, his images primal and child-like. It soon became apparent to Dan that he was re-creating something, an attempt to explain what happened to him during his NDE.

"I keep waiting for this compulsion, the energy, to stop," he says, "But it never does. It's all just coming through me and I've got to stay out of the way." In a comment similar to Bob's, Dan says, "The less I think of it, the better."

Dan sees art in his dreams. "The dreams start and then the anxiety builds. Then I'll make art for months straight. I paint five pieces at a time, since I can't wait for one to dry. In my dreams, I'll be in my basement, pulling things out and putting them together. Stuff that cognitively, in my waking life, I probably wouldn't do. And the next day I just go down there and start pulling it all together."

People bring Dan scavenged materials, which he stores in his basement, to use in his art. His process is primal, his materials primitive and elemental. His work includes found objects, archetypes, and images from his NDE, spirituality, and the natural world.

Dan thought he was "going nuts," as he puts it, because he'd never created art before. In fact, his degree is in geology. "I do what I do because of my NDE and I just try to keep myself out of it as much as I can," he says. "I was always worried that if I over-thought what I was doing, I would stop doing it."

Like Bob, Dan learned that he is only a vessel for expression from the universe. And like Evelyn (see the Preface) and Lewis, he learned to let his intuition guide him. *To get out of the way.* Dan allows the information to come from elsewhere. But where is it coming from?

Because Dan lives in Louisville, we agreed to a reading on Skype. I explained that we'd be able to see each other and interact as if we were sitting across the table from each other, because energy exists everywhere and distance is meaningless.

By now, I'd done about a dozen readings. My opinion of NDEs was shifting and my search to understand the cognitive and physiological after-effects was morphing to include wider areas. Spirit was taking me into other realms, showing me things I hadn't considered when I first began this work. I realized with a jolt, that I, too, was being transformed.

Dan's Session

Later that day, I dialed Dan on Skype. As the reading began, I looked outside. A storm was picking up; the branches of the trees on my porch were shaking. I closed the windows and took a seat at the kitchen table. Even though the weather was ominous, I wasn't worried about the electrical effect on recording Dan's session. The interference from the storm might turn off my internet, cable, air conditioning, or lights. But a storm creates a different level of interference than an NDEr, who can interrupt our internet connection while keeping other connections intact.

After a quick chat, I grounded myself. I closed my eyes and settled in to my higher consciousness. After taking three deep breaths, I began.

First I looked at Dan's aura, which was *solid from his head down—as if his body was strong but his head was complete consciousness. The aura surrounding his head was completely open and filled with white light. The white light of spirit.*

We moved on and asked, "What kind of person was Dan prior to his NDE? Did his upbringing, biology, or life experiences impact his NDE?" What we found was not surprising, in that Dan's experience mirrored others. Prior to his NDE, Dan was a person outside the everyday world. Spirit said:

Before his NDE, Dan and his wife were always living on the edge, where they felt most comfortable. They traveled to Africa, to South America and finally to Mexico, where Dan and his family fell ill. They were explorers, always looking for the next new thing, far off the grid. Beyond the mainstream. The more extreme the better.

Like Bob, Evelyn, Lewis, and others, Dan felt there had to be more—more to our reality on earth than what we experience. Yes, he was searching. But his journey didn't end until his NDE.

So was Dan a candidate for an NDE because he was an explorer? Because this was the ultimate exploration—one he would never find anywhere on earth. Was Dan set up for it? Was he, somehow, intended for his experience?

Prior to his NDE, Dan continued to go down a path, saying, "I want to know more about these things that no one understands, that we don't have answers for." He continued to pursue alternatives—in his case, new destinations—outside his comfort zone, until his NDE in 1991.

From what I observed and heard many times, experiencers like Dan and others seemed to think: "Give me something that's out there. I'm up for it."

But maybe an NDE was not exactly what they were thinking of?

What about timing? Is timing a factor in an NDE? When we asked this question, I saw Dan's consciousness flung from his body at the precise moment when Spirit determined that he was ready to incorporate this new experience into his life. When his life path was in alignment with the universe's desires, Dan disconnected, to be held in the palms of the universe, in utter perfection.

As we've seen, there seems to be a turning point, a particular time, when NDEs occur. This seems to be when people in situations similar to Dan's reach a certain point, an exquisite point, at which they are ripe for consciousness to be pitched from their bodies. A point at which their seeking overwhelms their reality. At the same time, a physical force is often present, to pave the way for the NDE to be activated.

Again and again, Spirit said: *At a certain point, they are pulled out of their bodies to be awakened and to return to carry on. On a different path. A path of higher purpose.*

Dan's experience left him with a gateway into a reality unlike anything he experienced in his former life. This paradigm shift, he says, was, "more real than reality itself."

Why is that? Others, like Barbara (see Chapter 3), mentioned that the reality of the experience was an especially strong feature of the NDE. We'll explore this more in later readings.

What Is the Meaning of Dan's Art?

Dan's artistic gifts have served as a catalyst for the rest of us. Many people who view his art are brought to tears or moved to relate their own experiences to him. Dan allows individuals to suggest their own interpretations and find the meaning of his work for themselves. Dan's job is to deliver the message and step aside. He remains in the background, merely the conveyance mechanism for enlightenment.

How does Dan explain his experience? What does Dan's NDE mean to him?

Dan says, "I had this experience that I don't understand, and it completely changed me. I was no longer the person I was born as. How do you communicate that to people?"

The point is, Dan communicates this through his art. Yet even as an artist, Dan's art is not conventional, but rather an unpacking of his consciousness. It's art he receives for the purpose of communicating a message. It's his way to explain the inexplicable, and to get around telling us anything directly.

Dan's mission is to act as a light for humanity. Indeed, he was sent back to imbue his higher consciousness in others. It's not a pact he made on his own. Unlike Lewis, Dan wasn't given an obvious mission. He doesn't remember being told that he would do this work. It's a compulsion he believes he must fulfill.

Opening the Door to Consciousness

What happened to Dan's consciousness during his NDE? How was it activated? These were questions we sought to understand as the reading continued and I attempted to go where Dan had gone as a cosmic traveler.

Imagine Dan's consciousness as a balloon lightly tethered to his body by a fine cord. During his NDE, this cord drifted farther away, yet was still lightly attached to him. That cord—sometimes referred to as the silver cord—is referred to in art and religion; it's discussed by mystics as the life thread that connects the higher self to the physical body. Dan uses that metaphor of floating and a cord as an integral part of his art.

We need that cord of consciousness to be connected to our body. It's what makes us human. If that cord is severed, there is no more you, at least in terms of the physical "you" on earth. The essence of you, the light, the energetic "you" exists forever.

"And in my art I manifest that tethering," Dan says. "I use that term a lot and manifest that tether as two chains dangling down to keep me from floating away."

What About a Life Review?

It's often assumed that NDEs include a life review, but Dan did not experience one. Nor did he see a light, or have a sensation of going down a tunnel. He was just floating away in darkness and was told, "You understand you're dying now?"

Dan had some concern about his lack of life review and the darkness he experienced. Why didn't he see a light? Why was there no tunnel? Because Dan didn't experience these elements, he was worried that perhaps his experience wasn't "valid." He even wondered what was wrong with him.

According to Spirit, Dan experienced everything he needed to, to convey the full meaning of the experience. To leave him with the results and the after-effects. The message was effectively delivered in the most appropriate means. *The universe knows what it's doing.*

In Dan's case, one sentence—"You understand you're dying now?"—combined with the rest of his experience, was sufficient to alter his life.

The way Dan made decisions prior to his NDE could be called "technical," as one might expect from a scientist. His wife was the family metaphysician, Dan says. But Dan experienced a U-turn after his NDE. Spirit showed me that the metaphysical part of Dan was always there, but locked up inside of him. The door to those spaces within him had been closed. Prior to his NDE, Dan thought, "This is who I am. This is what I do," excluding other possibilities.

But there was another part of Dan—a part that was there all along—that had the ability to interact with so much more. When Dan had his NDE, his experience broke down all the doors he thought he had permanently closed. After his NDE, Dan no longer had control over opening and closing those doors. Because once you've had an NDE, you never have anything under control again.

Transference From the Universe

Dan returned from his NDE with an overload of metaphysical force—a dose too big for him to manage. He has to work it off. And as he works it off, something unusual happens: It builds up again.

Here's what Spirit had to say about this: *Consciousness has its own life force. Almost as if it's fueled by a universal force. As Dan's consciousness is depleted, it refuels. As Dan burns it down, it builds back up. Dan produces art and uses it—but never uses it all up. It's powerful. It's Divine. Divinity. Dan's overload exists because the door he opened in his NDE remains open. Dan receives automatic refills, whether he wants them or not.*

People who haven't experienced an NDE have consciousness that is latent, that hasn't been activated like Dan's. We asked Spirit why consciousness is so responsive, particularly after an NDE.

The more you exercise your consciousness, the more responsive it becomes. The more you use it, the more it responds by coming back for more. Consciousness is very responsive.

"That's exactly the way it feels to me," Dan says. "You know, people say, 'Are you going to run out of ideas?' but no, because as soon as I go to sleep, it starts all over again. Everything comes from my dreams. It can be exhausting."

Dan's consciousness—our consciousness—knows all. It's part of the universe. It's all being. All knowing. It's of all time and space. It's everything and beyond. So when you go into that space in an NDE, your consciousness is accessing anything and everything. Because consciousness can. Because that's what it is.

When Dan's consciousness explores the universe, Dan is in the front row. One night he may be doing Shamanic activities, the next night he's having a dream about a bottomless lake, and the following night he's out in the universe. Because consciousness can do anything and be anything and be anywhere, all at the same time. It's alive. It's a living thing and it expands through a cycle of nourishing it.

"In terms of the dreams I have, it took a long time until I could even ask myself questions. And I came to the conclusion during my NDE, the door, my subconscious, was opened and I was thrown into my consciousness. And when I came back, that door just stayed open and didn't close. And that was really difficult. People never experience that, so it's hard to explain what your life is like," Dan says.

Dan went on to explain the first time he made a work of art: "As soon as I got out of the hospital, I made my first piece of art. A woven piece. I didn't have access to art materials but I would collect things in the desert. Found objects. I don't have any explanation for it. Did I tell you about it? It was when we moved to Tucson."

Tucson. There is was again. What was it about Tucson? This wasn't the first time that city had come up in my work.

"Where are you from originally?" I asked Dan.

"Oh, I'm from Baltimore originally," he said.

Baltimore. Where I live.

Primordial Art: NDEs and Their Links to Earliest Man

I've spent a lot of time thinking about Dan's and Bob's art and the significance of their work, including their techniques. Based on historical research, it appears that the art process of primitive man is surprisingly like Dan's and Bob's.

Dan's art shares a cultural space with cave paintings. Like the cave paintings at Lascaux in France, Dan uses primary pigments: red. Yellow. Black. His interest in color and form is similar to the Neanderthal signs of expression. The primary pigments used were iron oxides for red and manganese for black, and ochre created a variety of yellow shades. Dan's colors mirror this. If you look at Dan's paintings, you will see intense yellows, cadmium reds, and black lines.

Paleolithic societies interpreted their understanding of the universe through drawings depicting Shamanic journeys to other realms. Stars, symbolic elements, images from the galaxies. Both Dan and Bob make use of these symbols in their work. In Paleolithic art, many of the "upper world" images are drawn in red, associated with life. The images of the "lower world" are painted in black, associated with death. Dan's images mirror these styles as well.

"I feel like I got thrown into that part of subconscious that was prehistory, pre-religion and early," Dan says. "Cave dwellers. Shamanic."

Before the dawn of civilization, primitive man would smear raw materials onto crude surfaces. Paintings scrawled onto cave walls were probably made with a mixture of scavenged material and minerals, much like what Dan and Bob use in their work. The medium was crude, as were the paint elements, which were simply applied in rough, rudimentary strokes. Like our Paleolithic relatives, these two NDErs make use of rudimentary mark making, rough edges, and scavenged objects. The language of their work is simple, colorful, and primitive. Could Dan's and Bob's work be a link to man's earliest creativity? Both make use of elemental symbols and materials, and even the identical colors and workmanship as our ancient ancestors.

Both Dan's and Bob's art employ archetypal images and elemental palettes, that trace back to the origin of the species. If you put their work side-by-side with ancient cave paintings, you will notice the eerie comparison. Are their gifts evidence of the genetics of earliest man? Is their work a link between the ancients and our present-day society?

Cave dwellers applied the paint by blowing through a tube or directly from the mouth. They also used brushes made from animal hair or plant material, along with their fingers and rocks. Did Dan know that cave dwellers painted with plant material and their fingers, the same technique he uses?

Early man was not the only human to express Spirit through art. In later years, Shamans contacted the spirit world to develop images through altered states of consciousness, dreams, and visions. Like ancient Shamans, Bob and Dan both receive many of their visions in dreams and through altered states of consciousness.

We could certainly ask: Are Bob and Dan modern-day Shamans? We could also ponder the link between their language, their technique, and earliest man. These remain open questions, but the resemblance to the art produced by our ancient ancestors is uncanny.

"You can follow my art and it has everything you are talking about," Dan says. "It includes a Shamanic concept of the ladder and working toward Shamanic healing, parts brought back to make a whole person." Bob's work also includes ladders, images of healing, and symbols of the universe.

Remember that neither Bob nor Dan studied art. Neither trained as an artist. Both were scientists before their NDEs. Yet both are now compelled to produce art, and not just any kind of art. Cosmic art. Shamanic art. Are Bob and Dan embedded with a permanent memory from early man? Do they represent man's development of consciousness? But what type of realms—and how many—did Bob and Dan access? What message are they trying to impart to the rest of us?

When Dan and I concluded our reading, he said, "If you can, you should try to come down to Louisville to see the art. It's not the same as seeing it on a Website."

"I'd like to do that," I said, wondering when I would possibly be able to make that trip.

Little did I know that within two weeks I'd be in Louisville for the first time.

7 ✳ Lyla and Cognitive Transformation: ✳ Composer/Songwriter

> "After silence, that which comes nearest
> to expressing the inexpressible is music."
> —Aldous Huxley

As I walked through the wooded path in Robert E. Lee Park, I thought about my conversation with my friend Kitty. The previous week she suggested I'd join her at a presentation she was attending later that month. Kitty explained that it was a private group of open-minded friends who gather monthly for an interesting program or discussion. "You have to be interesting, interested, and open to be part of the group," she added.

"I'm interested," I said. "So, what's the talk about?"

"Aliens," she said, quickly adding, "Oh, did I mention it's in Louisville?"

I stopped walking. Of course it would be in Louisville.

A week later, Kitty and I made the 10-hour trip to Louisville. I planned a visit to Dan's studio (see Chapter 6), along with attending the meeting of her smart and open-minded friends.

I was digging. More experiencers were coming forward, including several "New Age" musicians who contacted me through the Website I'd set up to let experiencers know about this work.

New Age Music and the NDE

I enjoyed New Age music, but exploring it through the NDE led me on a journey to discover what feelings sound like. I discovered that New Age music is a wonderful way to not only relax but to touch others. Whether you find elevation, comfort, or hope in New Age music, the sound is able to fill the soul and bring on higher states of consciousness.

New Age music is primarily instrumental and meditative in nature. The music often takes its inspiration from the universe—the ocean, space, nature, or natural vistas. It's non-traditional in nature and can feature percussion including flute, bells, didgeridoo, and non-Western instrumentation. Some composers even build their own instruments.

You probably hear New Age music when you're having a massage, at a yoga class, or in meditation. Sometimes it's background music for weddings or video clips, and some New Age musicians create albums for healing or Pilates.

New Age music features melody at times, and strong rhythm and harmonic structure at other times. Virtually all New Age music employs repetitive rhythms, patterns, sounds, and drone-like qualities that are meant to convey a transformative experience. Even if you don't understand music, most of us can relate to New Age music's relaxing vibe. As Russian composer and conductor Igor Stravinsky once said, "I haven't understood a bar of music in my life, but I have felt it."

One New Age musician I spoke with told me how he began to hear music in his mind—telepathically—before he began composing music. He didn't know where it was coming from but it sounded wonderful and melted his heart. "I knew it would be spiritually uplifting for a lot of people if I could externalize it and manifest it so other people could hear it," he said.

I discovered that one New Age musician lives near Tucson and had a near-death experience but never spoke about it. Once again, I couldn't help but notice that Tucson had shown up and I wondered again about this connection.

Although this musician, who I call Lyla, didn't talk about her NDE, she created music—compulsively—day and night. After her concerts, Lyla goes straight back to her studio to work. Like other NDE artists, her compulsion drives her work and she is never without inspiration.

I emailed Lyla but I didn't hear back. I wasn't surprised. A month later I tried again. I left my number and asked her to contact me if she had an interest in speaking. Shortly afterward, the phone rang and it was Lyla. As I set up a pad of paper to take notes, she told me about her experience and mentioned she would be speaking about her NDE for the first time in Tucson the following week. She invited me to come and listen.

A week later I was on a plane to Tucson. Although I had come down with a cold a few days earlier, I decided to make the trip anyway. I stalled for a few minutes at the airport, seriously wondering if traveling was a good idea. Once I was on the plane, I reviewed my notes and listened to Lyla's music, and found a peaceful space during my harried trip.

The next day, I woke up from a nap in my hotel room, still woozy. I couldn't immediately remember where I was. Then it came to me: I was in Tucson to hear Lyla talk about her NDE. Realizing I was late to the talk, I dragged myself out of bed, rushed to the lobby, and jumped in the car. Ten minutes later I was in front of the community center where the talk was being held. I circled the block, passing the cars lining the street, and found a parking place at the far end of the lot. I later learned that more than 150 people attended Lyla's talk that day.

As I entered the center, I scanned the lobby. My eyes traveled from the registration desk to the book table to the posters on display. I maneuvered through the lines of chairs to make my way to the stage. No sign of Lyla yet.

I slid into a chair and waited, scanning the room every few seconds. Just when I was ready to give up, I noticed her at the far end of the room setting up her equipment. She looked like I imagined her, her slight form in white jeans and white shirt. She moved silently, adjusting her equipment, which she would use later in her talk.

A few minutes later, Lyla began speaking about her NDE, which had occurred decades earlier. Unlike some experiencers, she was not practiced at telling her story. Yet there was a certain rhythm to her speech—a beautiful language, full of movement and pattern, like her music. The audience quieted as they listened to her trance-like music, which had the effect of transporting them to an alternate realm, enabling them to visualize entering a portal to another reality. One listener said, "She's so far ahead of her time, that she's timeless."

The Curious Musical After-Effect of the NDE

Although Lyla didn't experience many elements of an NDE, she did undergo profound, long lasting after-effects, which altered her life and continue to drive her behavior to this day.

Lyla was shown an alternate reality that transformed her life forever, starting as soon as the day after the accident that led to her NDE. Her trajectory was fast and steep. Although she had absolutely no background in music and never played an instrument of any kind, she took a giant leap forward, to create ambient music to help people raise their consciousness.

Like other NDErs, Lyla figured she had nothing to lose after her accident. It's a common thread: NDErs are simply not afraid of taking a risk. "What's the worst that can happen?" one of them told me recently. "I already died."

I was intrigued by Lyla's "sound" experience and wondered how the music she creates is connected to the NDE. And what is it about New Age music that makes it a pathway to the higher mind?

Lyla's music falls in the category known as "trance" or ambient music. Listeners claim to experience heightened consciousness through its extended atmospherics. As one new Age musician puts it, "From the get-go, the intention of the genre was more about effect or feeling as opposed to the actual instruments used." Composers of trance music purposely set out to put the listener in a different state of mind. Interestingly, the root of the word *trance* gives us a clue to the meaning of this type of music: In French *transe* means "passage (from life to death)," the Latin *transire* means "to cross over," and the Scottish *trance* indicates "a passageway."

I always knew that music had the ability to transport us to another realm. My mother was a pianist and would play the piano in our living room when my brother and I were growing up. We would stop whatever we were doing and drift into the room to listen. I play the piano and have experienced the same effect, including the unusual reaction when my cats come to sit in front of the piano in silence. It's as if something unseen has entered the room—and perhaps it has.

The Ancient Elixir of Trance Music

The use of repetitive rhythms and sounds to induce altered states is an ancient phenomenon. Natural forms of percussion like clapping, or striking rocks, shells, bones, gourds, or sticks, induced trance-like states in ancient tribal cultures. And the low-frequency sounds of drums and rattles, bells, and gongs, have been used in Native American and Far Eastern ceremonies dating back thousands of years.

These identical repetitive sounds and patterns are all found in today's New Age music. Like the sounds of ancient cultures, today's New Age music possesses the ability to disable cognitive functions. The softer sounds of nature, the melodies of classical music, and the vocals of pop, can't achieve this. New Age music, with its repetitive rhythms and sounds, allows our minds to rest and guides us to higher states. This type of music fills up a space in our minds to deliver an experience of consciousness.

After examining the role of pattern and sound and its connection to altered states, it becomes clear why NDErs such as Lyla would seek out New Age or trance music following their NDEs. To put it simply, like Bob and Dan's art (see Chapter 6), Lyla's music is a way to convey what happened to her through a universal language.

Vibration and Sound: The Transformative Properties of Sound

We live in a vibratory universe and sound is a pathway to the reality we call higher consciousness. The gift of New Age music is to reproduce that sound—that humming of consciousness—to provide meditative or relaxing states. Music like Lyla's offers that transcendent reality to its listeners.

In coming chapters we will further examine the properties of pattern, sound, and rhythm. These properties, which we take so much for granted in our lives, are all part of the connective tissue that make up our world, and also happen to be key ingredients of the NDE.

Stepping Back: Examining the Reality of the NDE

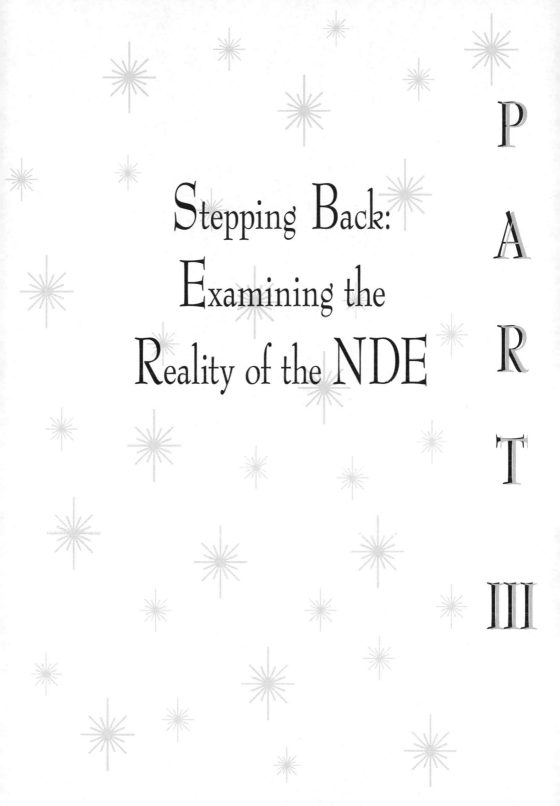

PART III

8 ✳ *Why You Don't Want to Experience an NDE* ✳

"Who is the wisest man? He who neither knows
or wishes for anything else than what happens."
—Johann Wolfgang von Goethe

When people hear about the research I'm doing into NDEs, they often ask, "How can I have one of those?" NDEs sound so appealing.

I must confess I'm mystified by the desire for this experience. After working with NDErs, hearing their stories, and learning about their lives afterward, I just shake my head when I'm asked this question. I often think that perhaps I didn't do a very good job of explaining this phenomenon. "Be careful," I always say. "Having an NDE is serious business."

An NDE is not just a simple matter of boosting dormant ambitions. It's not a reversible thrill ride, and it's certainly not a so-called walk in the park. The experience entails permanent and hazardous separation to another realm, and there's no turning back. In most cases, it involves nearly dying.

And that's not the least of it. There are problems when experiencers return—problems that can't be corrected. An NDE can bring on baffling, frightening, and even dangerous after-effects. If you listen to an account of a personal journey, you'll hear one story, but if you peek behind the curtain, you'll hear another.

I've talked to many men and women who have spent years trying to adapt to the new world they were thrust into. According to research by P.M.H. Atwater, it takes experiencers seven years, on average, to become accustomed to the changes brought on after an NDE.[1]

One after another, experiencers related how they quit their jobs, left their spouses, contemplated suicide, embarked on self-destructive behavior, and questioned their lives, following their NDEs. Physical trauma—chilling enough—is only one aspect of the experience. The emotional and mental burden is where things gets sticky. In this book, as you read the cases, no doubt you were thinking, "Why, they're prodigies! What I wouldn't give to have some of that!" But let me assure you: You're only looking at the silver lining of a very dark cloud. There's a price to pay for the experience. Here's why.

Most experiencers return with a sense of isolation. They've changed to their core. And it's not the kind of shift you can easily adapt to. It fundamentally reprograms you, and there's no way to get back to the old way of life. No how-to books to consult, no magic pill to take.

Dan Rhema (from Chapter 6) says, "I continue to feel like an outsider after the experience, as if I'm observing my life. When we lived in Tucson, I even asked my wife if I was a ghost, because I had the sense I wasn't really here."

A lot of experiencers feel similar isolation. You might be able to tell your friends or family you went to heaven and met God or had a conversation with your dead grandmother, but if you mention that you now get psychic messages and see dead people, the conversation stops.

Then there's the matter of your spouse. You stop eating the types of food they prepared. You no longer want to watch that favorite television show. You don't tell them that when you're standing in line at the supermarket or department store, you know what everyone else in line is thinking. You learn to keep your mouth shut. Your spouse asks what's wrong and tells you, "If you only stayed the way you were, we'd be fine." But you can't. It's impossible. According to one study at the University of North Texas, 65 percent of NDErs eventually divorce.[2]

But wait—there's more.

It's also common for the people you love to simply refuse to accept what you are telling them.

Then there's the issue of mission. Many NDErs know they were given a purpose during their experience, but don't remember what it is. The more fortunate ones recall and, if they're lucky, it's a mission easily applied to earth: music, art, a form of healing. But many have no idea what they are supposed to do now. All they know is they're meant to do something, but darn if they can figure out what it is.

Many spend years wandering, struggling with life purpose. Others crisscross the country, seeking an unfathomable answer. Some take odd jobs. Or no jobs at all. Many experience money problems. They think the next place will provide a solution to their very deep dilemma. Many never find the answers they seek.

Then there are the experiencers who had their peek into the metaphysical realm and found it the most profound and beautiful experience they've ever known. It offered so much more than this existence. It's not discussed often, but suicide is actually common among certain groups of NDErs. They long to return to the world that was so beautiful and perfect. And they believe they don't belong anywhere, anymore.

Time—keeping track of it, losing their sense of it, operating within our earthly time frame—becomes problematic. "After the experience, right up to this day, I'm disoriented in time and space as if the NDE erased my capacity to deal with time on earth," NDEr Marissa said. (See Chapter 12 to learn more about Marissa.)

Many NDErs report an inability to show up when they're supposed to. I learned early on they have difficulty keeping a schedule or appointments. It takes patience to work with them.

NDErs are overly sensitive, too, including sensitivity to others' energies. This sensitivity can result in inappropriate boundaries with friends or family members, and even with complete strangers. This behavior can cause social problems, such as butting into conversations and saying improper things at the wrong time.

In Chapter 10, you'll meet Robert Bare, an NDEr with unusual physiological properties. Robert once mentioned to me, "Did I tell you about the lady who painted her wall Chinese Dragon Red?"

"No," I said, shaking my head.

"I was in a Wal-Mart, checking out, and I usually try not to let anyone distract me," Robert said. "But something told me to tell this lady in line that she painted a wall red."

"So I interrupted her and said, 'Excuse me, did you just paint a wall red?'"

"Yes," she said.

"Was it Chinese Dragon Red?"

"Who are you?" she asked.

"Then a voice said, 'Please tell her I miss her and love her.' So I did. I said those words, as I stood behind her in line. They just came out. Then I left and went out to the parking lot," Robert said, still trying to figure out what happened.

NDErs' sense of smell also may be different following their experience. Their physician may explain this new, unusual sensation as an "olfactory experience," something I'd never heard of before.

One NDEr described her frustration with "real" life: "I feel very frustrated when I have to read a book to get information, since I already had access to all information of the universe," she told me. This may sound unusual, but this experiencer really believes and feels this way.

Something as simple as a conversation with others can be difficult for an NDEr because much of that conversation now seems irrelevant. Many have difficulty communicating, trying to put thoughts into words. It can be a challenge to hold a conversation with NDErs, because many are scattered and can't hold a thought. Others have a hard time concentrating. Getting them to focus and read a book, or to stay on task—except for their compulsions—may be difficult. After all, part of them is out in the universe now. No time or space exists there.

Many others have experiences they decline to discuss—things they can't explain. For example, some trigger malfunctions in electrical appliances. Some have darker experiences they don't want to talk about. Experiences like visits from menacing people from the other side or being taken to other realms at night when they're asleep. Dark realms they'd rather not acknowledge or mention.

How does this happen? More to the point, what are they supposed to do with these experiences?

Those who are eager to experience an NDE should consider that, in my extensive research, *NDE after-effects are permanent.* You can't reverse them. They are with you forever, even when you sleep. You can't escape.

The Desire to Make it Happen

I suppose it's natural for all of us to wish for greater connection. Yes, searching for greater meaning is perfectly understandable. But let's be real: NDEs are not the answer and they're not something we can set off to achieve, at least not by the traditional means in the metaphysical realm. NDEs are not something you can achieve by reading a book. By watching a DVD or listening to a CD. By taking a class or through meditation or yoga. You won't get there by drumming or chanting. It's not possible. And the best I can tell you is this: You shouldn't wish for one. The effects of these methods may be useful to heighten consciousness temporarily, but they will never grant anyone the permanent after-effects of an NDE.

Bear in mind that integrating an NDE into your life is done with much difficulty, if at all. Individuals who learn about NDE gifts are not considering the realities of life on earth, and how essential they are to our day-to-day functioning.

All of us operate in this universe and intersect with universal consciousness every moment of our life on earth. But, NDErs are unique because they have merged with universal consciousness. An otherworldly consciousness takes over their lives when they return and they become in a sense, an appliance for the universe. One NDEr says, "So many things have changed! Life seems more complex now because I am aware of another reality that I include in my daily life. It's like having more work to do every day."

Still want one? Let's look at some other facts about NDEs.

Some Questions About NDEs

All NDEs are different, just as all people are different. Some people have major after-effects from a limited experience, and others have rich experiences with fewer after-effects.

Is it possible to have an NDE even if you haven't experienced the elements?

Yes. Many have nearly died and don't remember much, if anything, about the experience, yet return vastly transformed with significant after-effects. Soldiers in combat are an example. Many return profoundly changed, yet have no idea why or what happened to them. Near-death experiences in the veterans' community are largely ignored. If a soldier tries to broach the subject, he is denied benefits. In the halls of the Veterans' Hospitals, only those cases that are categorized as PTSD are treatable for insurance purposes.

Do you have to "die" to experience an NDE?

You do not have to experience physical death to have an NDE. A break with reality is necessary, but this does not always require physical death or trauma. Every case is different and no universal model exists. No single explanation exists for all NDE cases.

Are NDEs reported in other parts of the world?

Yes. In 2001, a study was performed in Germany by Dr. Hubert Knoblauch, of the University of Zurich, that revealed that 4 percent of the population experienced an NDE.[3] A study of the Australian population in 2005, as part of the Roy Morgan Survey, concluded that 8.9 percent of the population in Australia had experienced an NDE.[4] NDEs have also been reported in Japan, Scandinavia, South America, and worldwide.

Are people who experience an NDE more religious?

NDErs are no more or less religious than the general population. Individuals come from a variety of religious backgrounds, and NDEs occur among people from all races and religious/spiritual backgrounds, including agnostics and atheists.

Do children experience NDEs?

NDEs occur in both children and adults. Today, there are many accounts of NDEs among young children. Their experiences mirror those of adults, including visions of the afterlife. Animals appear to be more prominent in childhood NDEs and life reviews appear less likely, as many children do not have a long enough life to recall. Like adults, children remember their NDEs many years later.

Does the way you lived your life prior to a NDE have any impact on the quality of your NDE?

There appears to be no correlation between your actions prior to an NDE and the quality of the experience. No evidence exists linking a spiritually based life with a richer or more meaningful NDE. The same is true for a wayward person. He or she will not necessarily have a more harrowing NDE.

What about the cultural aspects of NDEs? Why do some people meet ancestors and others meet a religious icon, particularly one they can identify with?

NDEs are personal in nature, but they are also collective. NDErs appear to filter their experience through their personal culture. If they expect to see Grandma in their NDE, they see Grandma. If they expect to see Vishnu, they see Vishnu. Yes, if they are very religious, they may meet a religious icon, consistent with their religion or culture. Why?

We all seem to have a narrative we believe in, which is translated into our experience. Consciousness appears to play a role because each series of beliefs is personal to the experiencer. This constancy speaks to the perpetuation of consciousness. The ability of our consciousness to retain what is already known, manifests when an individual enters this altered state.

If they didn't make all the stops along the way—experience all the elements—is their NDE still valid?

The elements are the gateway to the NDE. These visual images provide a platform for the journey, which extends beyond seeing a bright white light, a beautiful landscape or traveling through a tunnel. Yes, that is part of the experience for some. But there is meaning beyond the visual images. The elements, the stops along the way, are not the essence of the NDE. The point of the NDE is the end destination—permanent transformation. No inventory of elements can create the type of person the universe is seeking.

* * *

The NDE is a type of hero's journey, but one in which experiencers have no say, as they're carried in the hands of the universe, to travel to an unseen destination and return with the light of the universe embedded within them.

$\mathcal{9}$ ✴ The Self-Supporting NDE Community ✴

"Part of the process in healing from trauma,
like recovering from addiction, is developing
connection and support with others."
—Stephanie S. Covington

How do experiencers take care of themselves after an NDE? What type of support is available to assist them during their rigorous adjustment period? Who can they turn to for answers to their questions and to guide them through a sometimes-harrowing period that may extend for years?

Compared to several years ago, when NDErs were mostly left to their own devices, the situation has improved. New organizations have sprung up in recent years so that IANDS (International Association of Near-Death Experiencers) is not the only resource available for experiencers.

One of the first hurdles that experiencers must face is figuring out what happened to them. Many experiencers are not aware they had an NDE. Most aren't familiar with the term *near-death experience*. All they know is that life has changed and they must find a new way of living. Most are at a loss as to what to do next.

According to the Near Death Experience Research Foundation, as many as an estimated 13 million Americans have experienced an NDE.[1] Because many don't speak about their experience, the number could be even higher. "It's risky to discuss NDEs. You have to discern who is ready to hear this information," one NDEr told me.

We don't know how many of these experiences are harrowing, joyful, uplifting, or otherwise, because reported information on experiences is limited. The science of studying and classifying NDEs is early and, in many cases, the information derived from these cases is only reported within the confines of the elements.

Oftentimes, it isn't until years later when they read or stumble across the definition "by accident" that they learn what happened. By then, they've spent years wondering why nothing makes sense anymore—why the old pieces of their lives don't fit. Only later do they realize they had a transformative experience. Yet, even with this information, answers are often elusive.

Many don't talk about it. Here's what one experiencer said: "For many years I didn't want to talk about it because I didn't know how. And, I didn't want to examine *how* to talk about it with words."

Taboos also surround this experience. Some people are reticent to speak up because they're concerned about being pathologized—that is, medically characterized as abnormal. These fears are behind the decision to keep the experience to themselves. Some haven't spoken to a single soul, not a close family member or friend, and most certainly not anyone in the medical community.

That said, once they speak about the experience, their sense of relief can be palatable, a sense that a burden is lifted. Speaking about the experience to a supportive group who accept that this could happen, is helpful. Speaking with a community that has an explanatory framework provides a means to control the experience and put it in context.

There is much room for advancement in the field of NDE self-care. With more resuscitations taking place and more individuals coming forward to tell their stories, greater attention needs to be given to helping people care for themselves afterward. Most find that even something as simple as affirming that the experience really did happen, is supportive. Recognizing that others have traveled this road can go a long way toward easing the difficulties.

The truth is, many experiencers are not aware of the handful of organizations that exist to meet, share, and talk about near-death experiences, the latest NDE research, death, and the afterlife. In addition, some of these organizations are populated by the curious public, titillated by the stories of the "paranormal." Indeed, only about one-third of the members of some near-death organizations are experiencers themselves, according to authorities at IANDS. Despite limitations, here are a few organizations:

NDERF (Near Death Experience Research Foundation; *www.nderf. org*) has an online site that provides a forum for the near-death community. NDERF was developed by Jeffrey Long, MD, and Jody Long, JD. NDERF's mission is to provide information and support on NDEs. NDERF collects data, hosts a community bulletin board, lists accounts from more than 3,700 experiencers, posts research and articles, and has an online bookstore.

NHNE (Near Heaven Near Earth; *http://nhneneardeath.ning.com*) is a network interested in "unraveling life's great mysteries." NHNE offers supportive videos, news updates, case studies, and a social network. NHNE also offers classes and speakers at its location in Sedona, Arizona. Its goal is to pool resources and talents to create a global community and network.

IANDS (International Association for Near-Death Studies; *www.iands. org*) focuses on the near-death experience through a network of local chapters worldwide. IANDS sponsors an annual conference and a quarterly newsletter. Its Website posts news, publications, research, and stories about NDEs.

ACISTE (American Center for the Integration of Spiritually Transformative Experiences; *aciste.org*) offers support through research and education for those who've had near-death or similar experiences. ACISTE was founded by a former IANDS president. A specific aim of ACISTE involves providing support throughout the integration stage when dramatic changes often occur. ACISTE offers support and discussion groups, conferences, training, and continuing education for mental health and pastoral professionals, life coaches, and spiritual directors. In addition, ACISTE conducts ongoing research and educational programs.

What Do NDE Associations Provide? How Do Experiencers Interact?

The NDE world is small. Most experiencers no longer relate to our world—a world of often-mundane activities, 9-to-5 jobs, and sometimes-not-very-meaningful pursuits. They have one foot on the earth and the other foot in the universe. They suffer from an overload of consciousness and don't know what to do about it. This overload interferes with their day-to-day life and their ability to think and plan.

There is enormous shame and embarrassment around the NDE, and the experience can be overwhelming and indecipherable to many. Add to that, experiencers may keep their experience a secret, even within their own relationships. Keeping secrets is exhausting and adds to the strain of the NDE.

Many experiencers find they have little in common with former friends and relatives. The old world may not seem very meaningful anymore. And who else understands this new issue facing them? Other NDErs—their soul mates—their companions on the journey. These experiencers meet and form lasting friendships based on their unique way of viewing and interacting with the world.

As I've mentioned, California is a hotbed for near-death experiencers. IANDS regional groups exist throughout California, in Santa Barbara, Orange County, Los Angeles, San Diego, San Francisco, and Marin County. NDErs often socialize and form relationships, friendships, and even marriages with each other. After all, who else understands them as well as someone else who went through the same experience? In that way, these associations are similar to other support and self-help groups (AA, or Al-Anon for example).

Under any circumstances, it's a comfort to know you're around like-minded folks and that conversations can proceed without preliminaries. When you're with like-minded souls, your experience and your journey are accepted and validated, so you share common ground. In this way, NDErs are like everyone else.

Here's what one experiencer said about sharing his story in a group: "Of course when you're sharing like-minded stories with like-minded people, a new connection is created. And afterward, that opening really stayed with me."

In regard to receiving support, another experiencer said: "A lot of pre-conceptions or old conceptions I had around this experience were shifted. It was a good thing. I wasn't going to be criticized or ridiculed or looked at through some kind of negative light."

The NDE is a learning experience for those who've experienced it. But it can also be a learning experience for the rest of us. We can think of this as another lesson of the NDE.

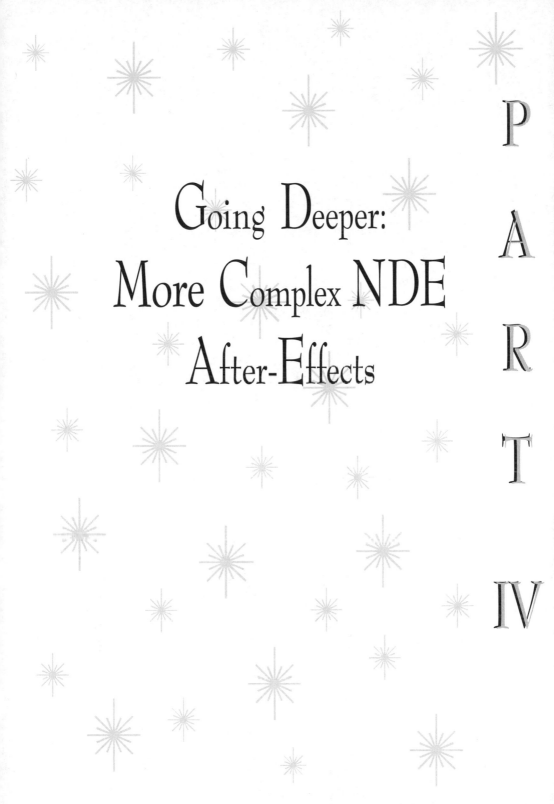

Going Deeper: More Complex NDE After-Effects

PART IV

10 ✳

Ken Ebert and Physiological Transformation:
Enhanced Hearing;
and Robert Bare and Physiological Transformation:
Enhanced Vision

✳

"Seeing, hearing, feeling, are miracles."
—Walt Whitman

Leaning back in my chair at Obrycki's, I looked down Pratt Street to Baltimore's busy Inner Harbor. I tore out a page from my journal and stuffed it in my purse, grabbed my car keys, and walked toward the garage. I was having dinner with a friend that night and needed to get going to meet her. She was including her cousin, who was visiting from New England.

My cell phone rang. When I answered it, it was my friend. She said that when her cousin found out that I was a psychic, she cancelled. I was dismayed but not shocked. This wasn't the first time I'd experienced a brush-off because of who I was and the work I was doing. *Does she think I'm going to cast a spell on her?* I thought.

I had been lulled into a false sense of security on the West Coast. In California, this work was fine. Being a psychic was fine. NDEs were fine. On the East Coast, it was altogether different.

I'd accepted that I couldn't change people's perceptions. Whenever you're doing something new and different, you're bound to encounter skepticism. And this work, with NDErs, as a psychic, was certainly different and unusual to some. I just had to keep moving forward. In a way, I was used to being a pioneer, someone treading new ground. It's something I've been doing for years.

As it turned out, back on the East Coast, I networked with even more experiencers. At that point, the doors were flung open, and soon I would connect with experiencers from all over the globe.

While surfing the internet, I read about Penny Sartori, a nurse in the UK. One of her intensive care patients begged her to let him die in peace. After this event, which shook her deeply, she began her research into NDEs. I contacted her and she wrote back: "I've come across a few cases where there have been interesting after-effects including the ability to hear conversations out of earshot. There is an interesting man in New Mexico, Ken Ebert, who is able to hear conversations from great distances since his NDE."

I looked up Ken on the internet and was surprised by what I discovered. I wrote back to Penny: "Funny thing is, I know Ken. I recognize him as a cashier at the local grocery store in Taos."

Penny replied: "Yes, Ken did use to work at the grocery store there."

Another coincidence?

I wrote back to Penny after I contacted Ken and told her I was in touch with him and that he remembered my face from my time in Taos. I thanked her for making the connection.

I knew Ken would be important to uncovering the key to the NDE, before we even spoke. Ken and I arranged to speak. He filled out the questionnaire and sent me a PDF of the book he had written about his NDE. I was re-connecting with Taos, my old stomping grounds. It seemed inevitable that this would eventually happen.

Enhanced Hearing: An NDE After-Effect

Ken Ebert had the type of after-effect I was particularly interested in. He could hear conversations at great distances. I remembered Ken as a soft-spoken man, someone who possessed an ineffable quality, as if he knew more than what appeared on the surface. I looked forward to speaking with him.

A week later, I poured myself a glass of lemonade and took a seat in my breakfast room. Stacks of papers, folders, and binders covered the table. I typed in Ken's number and hit the speaker button. I wanted to have my hands free to take notes. It rang twice, and then Ken picked up and began to tell me his story. I put down my lemonade as I listened. These are Ken's recollections in his own words:

"The accident happened in 1984. I was 18, living in the Florida Keys with my parents. I was biking and pulled back on the bike handlebars. The quick release mechanism on the front wheel gave way and I was flung off the bike. My face was raked across the handle bars and the gear shift levers and I was tossed to the pavement.

"I left my body and gazed down at myself lying on the road.

"At first I experienced darkness. Then a light appeared and I began to travel through a tunnel until I reached the light, which became a portal into a vast garden-like valley. The effect was synesthesia-like—colors were sounds and sounds were colors.

"A pure and powerful light-being, like a female guide who emitted intense light as part of her essence, met me in the valley."

At that point, Ken was given a choice to stay or return. He decided to return.

I took a sip of my lemonade as I waited for Ken to continue.

"When I re-entered my body, it felt too small to hold me, like being tangled in bed sheets. There was a snap and I immediately felt strong pain."

Ken was taken to a nearby hospital but turned away because of the severity of his wounds. He then was transported to a world-class trauma center 60 miles away.

After he recovered, Ken experienced several NDE after-effects that continue to linger. But by far, the most astonishing is the transformation to his hearing.

Ken's Sensitivities

Once Ken returned to his body, he experienced accelerated healing from the injuries sustained in his accident. His sensitivity to light and electricity increased. Light bulbs would blow out when he reached to turn them off or flare when he walked past. "I could actually physically experience light and heat as a pressure," he said.

But even more astonishing was the transformation to Ken's hearing. His hearing became more acute, but in a strange way. Sounds weren't louder, but if someone was talking about him at a distance, or even in a whisper, he could hear it, as if they were speaking against his left ear— always his left ear. His auditory range expanded in such a way that in a noisy crowd, such as a busy grocery store, he could pick out conversations from the other side of the room. Word for word.

Ken first noticed this shift when he was living in Boston a few years following his NDE. One day when he returned from work, Ken heard a high-pitched sound in his apartment. He walked through his apartment until he was able to pinpoint the source: the motion detector. But the system had never been armed.

After I spoke with Ken, I spoke with other experiencers with similar after-effects. One man could hear conversations in his neighbors' apartments in his large apartment building. A husband and wife, both NDErs, communicate between themselves in this way when they are separated. All of these experiencers only hear the sounds in their left ears. It is unclear why, but it may be connected to the fact that our left side is our "receiving side" for purposes of the metaphysical world.

Ken calls himself a "serial killer" of watches. But Ken's watches don't just die. There is a correlation among the times they died.

When Ken's first watch stopped, he put it on his newly built altar, something he created after his NDE. Ken then went out and bought himself a new watch. He wore his new watch for several months, and when his second watch died, he placed it on his altar. He noticed that the second watch died at the exact same time as the first one—except now the first watch was working again. Ken bought himself a third watch. The third watch did the same thing. It stopped at the same time as the first and second watches. Ken stopped buying watches after the third watch.

Ken and I made plans to have a session on Skype the following week. Ken was enthusiastic. He lives in Taos, was familiar with readings and all things metaphysical, and was looking forward to it.

Ken's Session

At 6:00 on Sunday night, I called Ken on Skype. He was already online, ready to go.

As I eyed Ken through my laptop's screen, I couldn't help but notice that Ken has the energy of a much younger man and, with his sandy hair and his interested attitude, he could pass for someone in his 30s. (Ken is 60.) Again, there was that eternal youthfulness NDErs seem to possess.

After I filled him in on how the session would work, we were ready to start. I pulled my hair back with a clasp and closed my eyes as I began to focus.

We asked about Ken's specific after-effect, his enhanced ability to hear sound, first. I wondered if Ken had any connection to the realm of sound before his NDE and I asked him straight out.

Ken had been classically trained in music since he was young. Sound and music were always prominent features in his life. Based on what we were told, it appears that Ken was given a boost to a feature that was already embedded in him. In a way, he brought back a heightened state of awareness of what already existed.

Because Ken recognizes electricity at times, we wanted to understand what was behind his electrical sensitivity. Here is what Spirit said:

Ken has to be "on"—cranked up a few notches, wired in a sense—for this to happen. And when he's cranked up—under stress in particular—the electrical connection in Ken reacts, causing a surge to his baseline energy. Ken's circuitry is then "switched on."

Based on what I was told through Spirit, Ken's reaction appears to be akin to a stress response, apparently stemming from the adrenal glands. One of the adrenals jobs is to produce epinephrine, giving the body the extra boost required in high-stress situations. This heightened emotional response produces a higher voltage energy, which feeds an already-energized state and creates a new, higher signal that interferes with our normal functioning. This form of electricity, which is prevalent in NDErs, has properties that go beyond electricity as we know it. It's energy at its highest channel, its highest frequency and vibration.

Ken acknowledged that when this electrical interference occurs, it is often accompanied by soreness in his lower back, where his adrenals are located.

In addition, Ken first experienced a dark place in his NDE and wondered what it was, and if other NDErs encounter a dark place. We asked that question next.

That dark space is the space between our physical body and the universe. Some experience the dark place when their consciousness initially exits their body, particularly if they have encountered physical trauma. Their consciousness hasn't yet transcended the world. It's passing through a low level physical state before it moves on to the higher vibration of the light.

I let out a long breath and asked, "What was the buzzing that Ken heard?" Spirit said:

When consciousness exits our body, its entrance into a higher frequency state creates what we interpret as a hum or buzz.

It's a different realm and we don't recognize the properties of that realm. We have no way of translating that process except to describe it as sound. It's a property beyond us. Like other properties of the NDE state, we are given a symbol or reference in our language even if that is not precisely the right attribute.

I felt a bead of sweat trickle down my back as I continued and Ken went on to relate his experiences with birds.

When Ken calls birds with his whistle, they come to him. At first I didn't pay much attention to his comment. Then I thought about birds and dogs and bats. They all have hearing beyond the ordinary human range. Why do these animals respond to Ken, like radar? Do they recognize his frequency as part of their language?

The human range of hearing is commonly 20 to 20,000 Hz. Perhaps Ken's range is now higher as a result of his NDE and is more attuned to that of animals with higher frequencies. Ken's frequency appears to have been boosted after his NDE.

"Ken was given a choice to stay or to return from his NDE. Why were Ken and others given this choice?" we wondered.

Making the choice interactive causes the experiencer to own the outcome, Spirit said. *They must take responsibility for their lives going forward and live in accordance with the universe once the choice to return has been made.*

Ken had personal questions about his life and work, and we chatted some more. Soon I realized we were done. I pushed the list of questions aside, thanked Ken, and signed off, as I gulped down a few swallows of juice. As usual, I had expended lots of energy in the reading. I reached for a Kind bar and thought about Ken's reading.

Ken was a willing participant and volunteered information that helped to put the pieces of the experience together. As was the case with others, there were aspects of his reading that were no surprise to him, that he suspected all along, but he was still interested in hearing another perspective.

And there were aspects that continued to confound him, such as the darkness he encountered and the extreme electrical reactions he has. I told him that because I was still doing research with others, answers to some of his questions were still likely to surface. Reading for Ken had produced a feeling of "going home," as Ken was a link to Taos, a place that felt "right." It felt right to connect with Ken, too, as more pieces of the NDE fell into place.

Robert Bare: Transformed Vision

Soon after meeting Ken, I received an email from Robert Bare, who had been referred to me by Mark Jacoby, the "man who talks to machines" (see Chapter 13).

A California highway patrolman for 22 years, Robert Bare worked the tough beats: East Los Angeles, Watts, and Oakland. Some of the most crime-ridden areas in California. Robert broke up demonstrations, gassed people, and beat demonstrators. After retiring from law enforcement, Robert worked as an adjunct professor and a city administrator, and served on two statewide boards of directors. He's worn many hats, but recently his life took another turn.

In 2009, Robert had a physical, which he passed with flying colors. Shortly afterward, he decided to visit his son and grandchildren for a week in Phoenix. When we spoke on the phone that first time, he recalled:

"The whole time I was there, it was extremely hot—100 degrees. I didn't feel well. 'Maybe I'm coming down with something? Maybe it's the weather?' I thought.

"I John Wayne-ed it all week. My son dropped me off at the airport at the end of my visit and I said my goodbyes. I told him how much I enjoyed his hospitality. At the airport I became nauseated but made it through TSA. I got on the plane and as I was loading stuff in the upper compartment, I just dropped dead."

Robert was deceased for 45 minutes.

Two crew members alerted the cabin crew that Robert had died from a heart attack. Firemen trained in CPR and a doctor were on board and, although they tried to revive him, Robert left his body twice as they worked on him. He recalled:

"I ended up in a tunnel and gravitated to this beautiful white light. I don't know if anybody was with me, but when I went into that light, it was just absolutely wonderful. I saw colors I've never seen on this earth. I lost track of time, like I was in an atmosphere where nothing matters. It was one of the most beautiful experiences I've ever had.

"I saw myself as a young person. There was a presence there, who was in control. This higher power, it was so humbling."

Robert communicated with another entity who asked him, "What good have you done in life?" A comprehensive life review followed in which he could see himself in all different stages, and see everyone else, too, and what they thought of him. Robert knew who said what behind his back and was exposed to every situation.

He said, "It's not a pleasant thing especially if you've had power in your life and you've done some things. It was hard to come back to life and see people and interact, but you have to move on and let go.

"It was the reckoning of my life. You feel everything; you're watching it, but you're in it, too. One thing I got from the life review is it seemed like you were judged by your actions and what you did and what you didn't do."

Robert doesn't recall if he was given a choice to come back.

About his NDE, Robert says, "I realized I could have done better. I did not want to judge or hurt anyone anymore. It changed my life, totally." Finally, he adds, "I only want to do good in my life. I mean that. I don't ever want to go through doing things that aren't perceived as good-hearted or good-natured or for the common good. I've always been someone who has an (extreme) AA personality and that's just not me anymore. It's not that I'm a bad person. I just don't want to be put in that position again. I don't live a day when I'm not appreciative and I don't live a day when I don't think it's not going to be my last."

Robert is now a grant writer for not-for-profits, charter schools, and disadvantaged children. He coaches softball and was named Citizen of the Year in his community in Oregon. "I take the time to enjoy things and relationships matter," he says.

Robert survived and went through an arduous recovery process but returned with several after-effects, the most remarkable of which is the improvement in his eyesight. Within five to six months, Robert's eyesight improved from 20/90 to 20/10—better than perfect. Four years later the improvement is still going strong.

✳

Robert's had other after-effects, too. He sets off the microwave when he passes. The fireplace turns on and off when he is near. And most strange, he says, "I can look straight ahead and it's like I'm in the middle lane. I see everything that is happening to me and I also see things in the fast lane and the slow lane. The stuff that's in the peripheral, it could be in the past, it could be in the future." In other words, Robert sees the past, present, and future simultaneously. "I remember the first time this happened. It floored me. I had a really hard time dealing with it," he said.

What Robert is experiencing is a psychic connection. When psychics receive information from the past, it enters on the left; in the present, straight ahead; and in the future, on the right. Robert is receiving his message through symbols, as all psychics do. The symbol Robert was given is a highway, which fits hand-in-glove for a former highway patrolman.

Robert's life before his NDE was chaotic and full of darkness. It was almost as if some force interceded to interrupt it forever to make his world crumble. As if they wanted to bring Robert into the light permanently. The timing was such that if this experience had happened to him 20 years earlier, it's not clear Robert would have had the maturity to deal with it.

I asked Robert if he felt he was increasingly going down the wrong path in his earlier years and he agreed. At times, he said, when he was faced with a fork in the road, he chose the dark path. However, Robert's come full circle from his time in the riot squad and those years of beatings and brutality.

Today, Robert's on a mission to do good. He sees himself as part of an interconnected whole with all beings in a life of service. He is fundamentally changed and I found, in the time spent with him on the phone, by email, and on Skype, that he was gracious, willing to spend as much time as he could to help out, and so sincere and emanating goodwill that I found myself having a hard time thinking of him in his previous life. Yet, when I read for him, I did see him in that life and knew that his former way of life was a fact.

Robert has gone beyond surviving the changes that occurred to accepting and transcending them. His new mind-set is a nudge from the Universe, which allows him to recognize that we're all in this together. Robert, in his small way, is contributing to the enrichment of our planet, as are the other NDErs you've met.

The After-Effects of Hearing and Vision: Light and Sound Waves

Ken's abilities were leading me deeper into the NDE vortex. To better understand Ken's incredible abilities, I turned to examining how hearing works.

Hearing, like other functions of the human body, is complicated, but let's try to look at it in layman's terms. Hearing is the ability to perceive sound by converting sound waves into vibrations detected by the ear. A pathway is formed from a series of bones and membranes that carries vibrations from our eardrum to the inner ear.

Our ears transform sound waves into electrical signals. Sound waves travel more slowly than light waves, but both frequencies are somewhat comparable—key data points in Ken's and Robert's similar NDE after-effects. Both Ken's and Robert's NDE after-effects share the properties of vibration and electrical waves.

The ability to hear is restricted mainly to vertebrates and insects. Within these, mammals and birds have the most highly developed sense of hearing—the two species that Ken's hearing was most attuned to following his NDE. Frequencies capable of being heard by humans are called sonic. Frequencies higher than sonic are ultrasonic. Bats are able to hear ultrasonic frequencies, as are dogs (the principle behind dog whistles).

Can Ken hear ultrasonically? And if so, why? And why would he need to?

Sound requires four components: vibration, a transmitting medium, a receiver, and an interpreting nervous system. Receivers, not only for sound but for other features as well, like vision, seem to be finer-tuned following NDEs. In Ken's case, he is able to hear higher frequencies. To know for sure what frequency Ken is able to tune into, we would need to measure the vibrations of Ken's ear in response to sound waves and electrical signals. For now, we have only anecdotal evidence of his abilities.

Yet, even without these tests, the clues were falling in place. I felt a twinge as I realized the connection in all these experiences. Even though energetic vibrations are not visible, they occur and produce much of our experience in life. The impacts of sound vibration, frequency, and waves were all fundamental to Ken's experience. And, these energetic properties appeared to be linked to Robert's experiences also.

Robert's After-Effect: Enhanced Vision

An understanding of waves and vibration is elemental to understanding our physical world. Much of what we see is only possible because of vibrations and waves. We see the world around us because of light waves. The same is true of what we hear. We hear the world around us by sound waves. If we understand waves, we can understand the concept of sight and sound. Both of these properties—enhanced light and sound—are also NDE after-effects.

Like other after-effects, it appears Robert's equilibrium state—in his case, his baseline vibration that gives him his ability to see—was disturbed by a tremendous force.

The human eye is able to focus light rays from various distances and convert them to impulses. When light strikes portions of the retina (millions of light sensitive cells), it's converted to an electrical signal that is relayed to the brain via the optic nerve. We can speculate that the conversion of this signal was somehow enhanced in Robert, which amplified what he receives. As with other NDE enhancements, we can hypothesize that the boost to Robert's energetic vibration, also incrementally improved his eyesight.

Similar to the change in Ken's hearing, Robert's equilibrium was disturbed, which altered his vision. In Ken's case, the process of the conversion of the signal as the ear transforms sound waves into electrical signals is similar to Robert's process with vision. Both Ken's and Robert's after-effects are tied to frequency, sound, and light waves. The NDE after-effects were coming into keener focus as the stage for the NDE blueprint was being set.

11 ✳ *Lynnclaire Dennis and Cognitive Transformation:* ✳
Sacred Geometry

"There is geometry in the humming of the strings.
There is music in the spacing of the spheres."

—Pythagoras

Winter arrived in Baltimore: 60 inches of snow, temperatures in the 20s, and shortened days that ended in an early, gray dusk. As winter set in, I thought about the artist's colony in Costa Rica I visited a few years earlier. Costa Rica, with its 80-degree days, palm trees, and green culture, sounded alluring as I looked out at the 3 feet of snow piled on my patio. I called the colony and they had space. A week later I was on a plane to San Jose.

The first week I swam in the retreat's icy pool and took strolls into town to pick up fresh pineapple and bottled water. In my simple casita, I sat on the plastic couch with the curtains closed and sifted through the list of experiencers I had brought along with me. One caught my eye: Lynnclaire Dennis.

Lynnclaire lives in Belgium and received sacred geometry in her NDE. When I emailed her, she asked that I call her on Skype. A few minutes later, I poured a glass of iced tea and dialed Lynnclaire's number. Here's a portion of what she told me:

"The way I was brought up, what you got when you died, your body was toast. You got six feet of dirt. If you lived the good life, you got the pearly gates and if you lived a good way, you got to go to heaven. There was no support for the paranormal."

Lynnclaire's NDE

Lynnclaire Dennis was living life in the fast lane at the time of her NDE. Divorced at 31, she was an average kid growing up. Her father was a minister. As a child, Lynnclaire went to church three times a week and later became a missionary with a collegiate organization.

She recalled, "There was nothing that led me to accept or believe in a near-death experience. I never heard of it until I experienced it, 27 years ago. It was something quite new. No one gave me a rational explanation for what happened."

In January 1987, while on her honeymoon, Lynnclaire Dennis died over the Swiss Alps. She lost consciousness in a hot air balloon as the pilot took the balloon to a level in excess of 20,000 feet without oxygen.

"I found myself outside the balloon looking down on my body. The next thing I remember was putting my foot down on Mt. Rainier in Washington State," she said. "Most people talk about going through the tunnel to get to the other side, but that was not my experience. All of a sudden, I'm no longer over the Alps. It's not January. It's July. The meadows are in full bloom, and my grandmother's coming to meet me. But my grandmother died when I was 11.

"It's still so real. I had a life review. A man communicated with me telepathically and said, 'Lynnclaire you will be a catalyst for change,' and then that person turned and walked out. The stage dissolved and then my father came out."

She paused and took a breath.

"Music drew me in to a tunnel of light and I realized I was looking at me. And at a strand of tapestry weaving all creation, a highly dynamic and luminous structure. I remember thinking, 'I'm going home.' Then, all of a sudden, the music screeched and someone pulled me backward through the tunnel. It was my husband, a physician, trying to revive me. As I was leaving, I looked over my right shoulder and realized that I had to remember the details of what I had seen."

Lynnclaire was later pronounced dead at the hospital.

"In earthly time, I was gone quite a while. They think I lost consciousness at 9,000 feet. I remember hearing the dialogue between my husband and the pilot. And during that time, I was having this very richly textured experience."

Later, Lynnclaire had recurring dreams about the pattern she had seen in her NDE. But it was a four-year process to remember the geometric angles of what she was shown. She became obsessed with unpacking her experience.

"I took paper and pencils and colored pencils with me everywhere and tried to reconstruct the pattern. It's music. It's light. It's how matter moves and it's love," she said. "Over time, we began to look at it more closely and discovered that this simple pattern, which is nothing, is a knot, a pattern of light, a vibration. It's about time and a connection between energy and matter."

Lynnclaire and I concluded our conversation and she agreed to send me additional information about her NDE and the Pattern. We agreed to Skype the following week. Within a few days, I was looking at complex descriptions of mathematical theory that she sent as I tried to piece together her experience. What did the Pattern mean? And why did Lynnclaire receive it?

The Pattern

As I explored Lynnclaire's experience, I learned that the Pattern relates to humanity, consciousness, and time. Some think the Pattern reaches back before the conception of the universe or relates to properties that go beyond the universe. There is some feeling that the Pattern represents the blueprint of consciousness—a model about how to think about form and pattern.

Lynnclaire has no background in mathematical theory or topology, an area that touches on DNA, genetic code, and chemistry. She was a minister's daughter with a background in sales. *There is no way Lynnclaire could know about the Pattern's cosmic and universal qualities*, I thought. Though she had no scientific training, the mathematical accuracy of Lynnclaire's intuitive drawings has since been verified by numerous scientists around the world.

The Pattern eventually caught the eye of quantum physicists because of its compatibility with superstring physics, the Holy Grail of all physics. One of the people fascinated by the Pattern is Dr. Louis Kaufman, who has been studying knot theory and topology for the past 30 years. According to Dr. Kaufman, "We search for fundamental patterns in math and physics. We ask questions about the nature of form, the nature of pattern. Everything we see has some pattern in it. Everything you have ever looked at in the world is a similar amalgam of form and content."[1]

In a 1997 interview, Dr. Kaufman spoke of discovering that the knot in Lynnclaire's Pattern can be "represented by pure frequency two, pure frequency three and a mixture of frequencies five and three. This vibratory pattern gives a good approximation to the shape of Lynnclaire's Pattern knot."

Lynnclaire works with a team of scientists from the University of Illinois at Chicago to mathematically describe the Pattern and has recently worked with NASA to further uncover the meaning of the Pattern.

Dr. Louis Kaufman had this to say about the unifying principle behind the Pattern: "Here is something that if you look at it one way shows you the Star of David, another way, it shows you the Yin-Yang. If you turn it again you see the crescents sacred to Islam and the symbol for infinity. And they're really all the same."[2]

Can this Pattern be used to guide relationships? Could it be a key to healing? Could it be an archetypal symbol and the foundation from which all that exists is created?

According to some scientists, Sacred Geometry allows us to contemplate the creation of the cosmos. It's not only involved in how we relate to the universe, but how we relate to time and how we've been created. What kind of strange alchemy brings together these higher-dimensional designs within the NDE? Does it represent a communication from beyond?

Sacred Geometry and the NDE

Other NDErs also recount seeing Sacred Geometry—all shapes as one—in their NDEs. One NDEr related viewing astonishing, upside-down *merkabas*—two interpenetrating three-sided pyramids that link the mind, heart, and body. These dramatic merkabas awaken, heal, and transform on the physical, mental, spiritual, and emotional levels, and also transport a body from one dimension to another. The merkaba's appearance in an NDE makes sense when viewed through what we know about the NDEs' transformational journey: a bridge from one dimension to another.

Perhaps the NDE itself is a kind of merkaba? A startling, multidimensional experience linking mind, body, and spirit.

Lynnclaire's Session
I sat on my porch overlooking the village of Cuidad Colon. It was early morning; the air was muggy and the sun bright overhead. I made a list of questions for Lynnclaire, and by the time I finished it was 10 a.m.—almost time for Lynnclaire's reading. I wiped the film of sweat off my neck and went back to reading my files. An hour flew by, and at 11 a.m. I looked up and noticed it was time to call Lynnclaire.

"Are you ready?" I asked as we began. I heard the crackle of electricity and other voices on the line as I repeated, "Ready?"

"Ready when you are," she said.

This was not the first time I heard other voices on Skype. I also heard them on my cell phone and occasionally on the radio. Who were they? Were they others Skyping or using their cell phones, and our lines were crossed? Or were they voices from beyond?

EVP (electronic voice phenomenon) is in the realm of possibility, given the high vibration created in these sessions (although we never determined with certainty what caused the interference in these conversations). In Lynnclaire's case, we lost the connection through interference 11 times during her session.

I took three deep breaths, felt myself turning inward, and quieted as I focused. I looked up as Lynnclaire waited for me to begin. I began by remarking on her crown chakra. "Your crown chakra is totally open," I said. The crown chakra is where Lynnclaire and all NDErs receive information. "The rest of your chakras are diminished because your entire electrical field is focused on your crown chakra. This is the chakra that drives you."

I discovered that most NDErs have very active crown chakras. The crown chakra represents our connection with consciousness, the meeting point between the body and the universe. The challenge for NDErs is to remain open to the universe while at the same time staying rooted to the ground. With a totally open crown chakra, this is another challenge of the NDE.

"My sense has always been that I'm not chosen but I had an opportunity and I chose. Is there a reason you can see that I was chosen for this NDE?" Lynnclaire wondered.

Like a whisper over my shoulder, I was told by Spirit: *"They" knew you would shoulder the work and this would become your life. This was key for why you were selected. Each NDEr returns with a road map for their journey and each map is unique but each of you creates a pillar of light that becomes unified.*

"What is the Pattern?" Lynnclaire asked. "What did I receive?" Even though Lynnclaire had worked on the Pattern with the help of science, she was still interested in Spirit's answer.

I spoke slowly as the information flowed in:

What you received is beyond the universe—properties birthed before the conception of the cosmos—properties that are eternal. Your experience is evidence that it is possible to communicate with the eternal by looking beyond.

"Why now? Why do we have the Pattern?" Lynnclaire asked, as I paused to take a drink from my water bottle and heard the steady drum of the stationary fan in the corner of the room.

Others have been shown or came upon the Pattern in other times and in other civilizations. One of these civilization went far. They're showing me pyramids in Egypt or Mexico. *One of these civilizations built pyramids or sacred sites and had very deep knowledge of this and got to the core of the Patten.* "They're showing me Mesopotamia," I said.

"Sumeria," Lynnclaire added, as I wondered about these connections.

Lynnclaire nodded and continued. "What is it that we do not understand about the universe and creation? What is the source of all?" Lynnclaire asked. "Will we get closer to mysteries like the Pattern yet never fully understand them?" I wondered what Spirit would say in response to Lynnclaire's complex question.

In my head I was shown images of stars, planets, and galaxies.

The ineffability of what I was shown made me stop. There are really no words to describe the experience and what I was shown at times in the readings. Not for the first time, I found myself in the shoes of the NDEr, searching for a way to adequately express the symbols of infinite knowledge and space, the colors and symbols. Symbols I couldn't adequately describe.

I looked up. Skype had turned off. I lost Lynnclaire. I redialed and Lynnclaire immediately answered. We remarked over the lost connection and went on. "What is the mission of NDErs?" Lynnclaire asked. Again, that question of mission. It was only a matter of time before Lynnclaire would ask.

Their mission and life path is imposed on them by Source. It's automatically imposed since their life has been taken out of their hands, Spirit said.

Lynnclaire had a few more questions about her upcoming book and her life in Belgium, and we chatted a bit more about Lynnclaire's family and living in Europe. We tried to think of a way to connect on U.S. soil and promised to stay in touch. We finished the reading, and I turned off my laptop and rested my head on my desk, cushioning it in the crook if my arm. I closed my computer and slipped my notes into a folder as I considered Lynnclaire's reading. The nonstop electrical interference had created many interruptions. Having a session interrupted so many times required careful checking to deal with the vagaries of the uncontrollable. I rechecked my recording device for the dozenth time and slipped my notes into my file.

Sacred Geometry

For a long time, I had certain ideas about how this NDE research would go. I assumed the work would fall into buckets and that each bucket would be explicable and discreet. Lynnclaire's abilities didn't fall into any bucket, at least not at first glance.

Lynnclaire, like other NDErs, returned from her NDE with talents based on age-old disciplines and newfound faculties that were uncannily ancient, yet also everlasting.

To sum it up, Lynnclaire's gift—Sacred Geometry—depicts the fundamental forms of space and time. Sacred Geometry employs pattern recognition and links universal templates used in the design of everything in existence, including architecture and art. Sacred Geometry is a fundamental truth, a philosophical and actual building block of all structures, manmade and natural, at both the simplest and most complex levels. Even cutting-edge technology employs Sacred Geometry patterns and language.

In the sixth century BC, mathematician Pythagoras led a school of thought that married geometry, mathematics, and music (all related to the NDE and its after-effects). Pythagoras believed that geometry and math held the keys to all life. The basic notion is that geometry and mathematical formulas, harmonics, and proportion are found in light, music, and creation—all revealed and tied throughout the NDE and its after-effects.

The Ancients, including the Druids, the Maya, and the Sumerians, integrated Sacred Geometry into their mystery schools. More recently, this doctrine was transmitted through the Vedic philosophy, Feng Shui, and Taoist principles. Leonardo Da Vinci used the proportions of Sacred Geometry, the intersection of science and spirituality, in his depiction of Vitruvian man, the image I was shown in Javier's session (see Chapter 2). The patterns I was shown in other NDEs—music, math, form, and color in art—all utilize Sacred Geometry. These patterns give the universe a specific power.

The standards used to measure our planet, the tenets of Sacred Geometry, arose in Lynnclaire's reading. What Lynnclaire received demonstrates that certain patterns are woven into the fabric of our lives. Recognizing this simple fact allows us to understand how this template of patterning was replete throughout all the after-effects. Musical patterns, the patterns of sound and light waves, the patterns of form and color in art and in math: All are representations of repeated patterns found in NDE after-effects.

Lynnclaire's after-effect, the Pattern—an energetic blueprint—served as a key of sorts for understanding NDE after-effects. A way to understand not only our metaphorical path through life, but also through the NDE.

Unlike other NDErs who received a gift that we recognize as a "talent," Lynnclaire received the key that unites all the after-effects and their repetitive elements. Lynnclaire's after-effect was an important explanation for the other after-effects, I realized.

But there's more. Lynnclaire's Pattern is useful to understanding the road map to the NDE, the cosmic key that unlocks the language of higher understanding. Lynnclaire's Pattern, the delicate and sublime, full of knots and links, the work of angels and a higher power, may be an example of ancient patterns and languages that have been retrieved from the universe, embodied in new messengers. But if so, can we understand the message and its deeper meaning?

12 ✳ *Marissa and Cognitive Transformation:* ✳
Musical Talent

> "Music is an echo of the invisible
> world."
> —Giuseppe Mazzin

I'd been sitting in my office most of the morning. I'd only come in to look for some papers, but soon the time had passed. It was only 8:00, but the winter sun had been up since 6:00. Girly Girl, my calico cat, lay curled up in a cozy ball next to my laptop. My cell phone rang and interrupted the peaceful silence.

"Hi! It's Marissa," a soft voice said.

I sat up straight in my chair. I hadn't been expecting her call that early.

Earlier that year, I'd spoken to an NDEr who was enthralled with music. He knew a woman who'd had an NDE and returned with a shift to a completely new talent. She had never spoken publicly about her experience, but he told me her account was complete with an identified mission to serve humanity. Because she didn't want her story told under her name, she chose the pseudonym Marissa. "I will know when I read about 'Marissa,' that I am reading about me," she said.

I opened a drawer and pulled out a legal pad as I pushed the cell phone against my ear.

I jotted down Marissa's words as fast as she was speaking them, concentrating on her story while managing to keep writing.

Marissa, a former director and writer for television documentaries, hadn't played an instrument prior to her NDE six years earlier. "I didn't have any musical background and never felt a calling for music," she said.

Life before her NDE was typical of a 30-something, single, professional woman. "If you're in your 30s, it's all about starting a family, having

134

a career, having others' approval, and finding a good husband," Marissa said. As a documentary producer, she was caught up in that world, and was herself a professional success by the age of 31.

While Marissa was traveling for work in Belgium, her lifetime battle with body image ended and she collapsed unconscious. Within moments, she experienced her NDE. Questions concerning planet earth, mathematical equations, scientific topics, astronomy, philosophy, and physics were all revealed to her and she was told the answers were "simplicity."

"My out-of-body experience happened immediately. My consciousness began to increase and I was thousands of times more aware and conscious then I am now. There are no words to describe the feeling of freedom," Marissa said.

"Go on," I said.

"I left my body and found myself in a small chapel in the tourist site where I was staying. I lay in the chapel. There were lots of tourists there and I could see all of them, as if I had peripheral vision. I recall thinking, 'I can't just lie down in the chapel. Everyone will see me!' But I was feeling so peaceful that I didn't care."

I waited for her to continue.

"I spontaneously returned to my room. As I got closer to my bed, I saw a person lying on their back. I didn't recognize who it was until I got closer and saw that it was my body, but not me. My consciousness was completely detached from my physical body, as if I was looking at a chair or another object.

"It felt like my consciousness was connected to a 'volume switch.' Some external force was gradually turning up the volume until my consciousness was infinite. Right after my NDE and for several weeks afterward, I was very confused because the reality/consciousness in which we live, seems like a dream. The reality of the NDE seems like the real reality. It seems like we only access only a very small part of a much larger reality on earth."

Other NDErs echoed this same sentiment. Our reality seems "thin," not complete, to them. Not even real.

Marissa recalled, "Next, I was sucked at a speed that is indescribable into a 'vacuum of love.' It was very pleasant, as if someone was looking after me to get me into a safe place. I clearly thought, 'I do not know what is happening, but I don't want it to end.'"

We sat in silence for a minute and then she continued.

"There was no sense of time or space and, in fact, time no longer existed. Up to this day, I am disoriented—as if something had been erased in my capacity to deal with time on earth. I find it very challenging to organize my agenda and I lose track of time easily."

I wondered if Marissa met anyone or encountered other beings during her NDE and asked her.

"After being left alone in this empty place, little stars began to appear—thousands of them. I was floating in space and felt connected to the universe," she said.

Other NDErs I spoke with also recount experiences with the stars: Dan and Bob, who re-create stars in their artwork (see Chapter 6). Evelyn, who is called outside to look at the stars at night (see the Preface). Mark Jacoby, who closes his eyes and sees stars (see Chapter 13). What is their connection with the stars?

Marissa came to a boundary and had to make a decision: "If I decide to move further into this beautiful cosmos, I will never be able to return to my body on earth. I remained watching the cosmos because it was so beautiful. I didn't know what to choose and was hesitating. Should I go ahead or not?"

Marissa returned to earth following her NDE, where finding simplicity was a challenge.

The year after her NDE was rough for Marissa. That first year, she didn't tell anyone about her experience. She herself didn't know what happened, but in her heart, she knew that something had changed. "The other side was so peaceful and full of love," she said, "and the sense that everything was so right was prevalent. Coming back to earth was a big shock because I knew something big inside of me had changed forever."

Uncontrollable Behavior After an NDE

After her experience, Marissa began to read about NDEs and to rethink her career. She realized she was not afraid of death and could be around people who were about to die. She wondered how she could serve.

Shortly after her NDE, Marissa went to visit a friend. There was a harp at her friend's house and although Marissa had never been interested in the harp, while her friend went to work and she was alone in the house, Marissa went outside with the harp and began to play. She couldn't imagine how powerful the sound was and was hooked right away. In fact, she had to stop playing because the sound, the vibration, was too powerful.

For two or three more days, Marissa stayed at her friend's house. Each time her friend went to work, Marissa spent more and more time playing the harp.

"I knew that when I returned home, there would be no harp," Marissa said. "I decided that if within two weeks, I was still interested in the harp, and missed the sound and vibration, I would make a decision."

When the two weeks were up, Marissa realized she needed that vibration. It was a real, physical need, she explained. "The harp is a very special instrument," she explained. "Although it's a string instrument, its vibration is different than a guitar or cello. The harp's sound is loving."

Marissa told me that she recognized that loving sound right away—a sound soothing to the soul, the sound she experienced in her NDE. Marissa made up her mind to buy a harp. There was only one problem: She didn't have any money.

She managed to find a secondhand harp for sale on the internet for $2,000. But Marissa didn't have $2,000. She recalled, "The strange thing was, months before this, I was working on a contract film production, doing script writing. I thought the contract was over and I had received all the money I was going to get from that contract."

Marissa spoke to the woman who was selling the harp and said she was very disappointed, but could not afford to buy the harp. The next day, Marissa got a phone call from the production company.

"Did you get the check?" they asked.

"What check?" she replied.

"We're very sorry," they said, "but it seems we're late sending the check out. We still owe you. It's a check. For $2,000."

That's when Marissa knew she was supposed to play the harp. She told me, "The weirdest thing was, I had no goal or ambition with this instrument. It was just that the vibration was so strong."

So Marissa bought the harp and put it in her living room and stared at it each day. She had no technique or plans, no goals or ambition for the harp. For weeks she stayed up late in front of her computer Googling "harp." One night, she typed in "harp" on Google and the last title on the screen was "music thanatology"—playing the harp for the dying.

Marissa read the sentence three times to make sure she was reading the correct words, and then clicked through to a web page. She was taken to an article about a very specific music therapy that uses the harp at bedside for patients at the end of life. "I cried and everything made sense then," she said.

Marissa didn't have the money to spend months in training for harp thanatology, but every time she needed money, money appeared. "I was very lucky," she said, "because somehow I got a tax refund." Not only did she receive a check, it was for the exact amount of money she needed for the harp intensive.

Before Marissa joined the bedside harp program, she called a palliative care residence and asked if she could come once a week to play the harp. She spent the last $25 in her bank account to drive to the palliative care residence, telling herself, "This is crazy. I have no money. I bought myself a very expensive instrument and I'm not even sure I can do this."

But from the moment she walked into the residence, she felt unconditional love—the same love she experienced during her NDE.

"It was like going home," she said. "As if someone was with me to do this work. It was an intuition so strong, you know you are not alone. I knew it was the beginning of a quest, a very important journey. I knew I would do this but that I would have help along the way."

When Marissa began her harp lessons, the first thing her teacher said to the class was, "This work is all about simplicity."

When she heard that, Marissa knew she was at the right place, doing the right thing, serving the right cause. "I have a feeling it's one of the most important things I've done in my life. It's bigger than me. It's more universal. It's bigger than the harp."

Marissa and I made plans for a session the following week. She had many questions about her experience, and the other, unaccounted-for experiences since she returned, when she is taken and shown things she doesn't understand and that frighten her.

Marissa's Session

I settled in at the desk in my office, adjusted the blinds in the room, and dialed Marissa on Skype. She answered on the first ring, and her youthful face with long dark hair appeared on the screen.

After a few minutes of arranging the volume I asked if she was ready and she nodded her head to indicate yes.

We began with Marissa's aura. Would it look like other NDE auras? Gauzy, filmy, and light-filled?

When I observed Marissa's aura, I noticed that Marissa had traveled—had been out in the universe. Through me, this information emerged.

Your aura is completely one with the universe. Your physical body was replaced by the universal source of All. The NDE was a way to be transported from our world to that higher world, of infinite ascent.

Marissa nodded and asked for more information. I heard her tapping on her computer as I continued.

For you and others, an NDE is if you are going from being slimly connected to the universe, to being completely connected to all the experiences we're unable to have on earth. Of course, anyone would want to return to that realm. You traveled to a realm which is neither earth nor the after-life.

Marissa was concerned if she was fulfilling her mission. She directly asked: "What am I meant to do on this earth?"

Throughout Marissa's session, there was—similar to during Lynnclaire's session (see Chapter 12)—a high-pitched, high-intensity sound emanating from the computer. I looked left. I looked right. I tried to ignore it and continue. I was learning that electrical interference was commonplace in all of my encounters with the NDErs.

Marissa's mission is to emit love and universal consciousness to all she encounters. She was intuitively guided to the harp, and through that, the answers were revealed to her. All NDErs seek out the vibration of the NDE on

139

earth, to reintroduce their pathway and reconnect to that illusive realm. The harp is Marissa's way to connect to her mission.

Marissa was a communicator in her former life as a producer/director/writer. Now she is also communicating, but on a higher platform, and to her, a more meaningful path.

"What was the love I encountered?" Marissa wondered. "It felt like nothing I've ever experienced."

I took a deep breath and listened.

When we're free of our physical body, we exist as perfect energy. Here, on earth, we call that perfection love. It exists over all, is benevolent and doesn't judge. It is the purest form of All. While it may be another property, we call it love.

"Why was I told the answer was simplicity?" Marissa asked. "Why was I given that message?"

If there is one thing that exists in all dimensions and yet—at the same time—in one dimension, that is love. It is simplicity itself. It contains everything. The one thing that contains all. That's the simplicity part.

She interrupted this explanation with a question. "Why did I have the sense that the reality of the NDE was more real than the reality of earth?" she asked.

I recognized this as a question that came up over and over from all of the NDErs.

The NDE is the gateway to the universe and infinity. On earth we cannot grasp this since we lack a context for infinity. We tend to view the NDE through the prism of our physical world.

I looked up at Marissa. She was smiling and nodding. I continued listening and relaying the information.

Consciousness is the only true reality. It's pure and complete. It contains all of the universes and everything that's ever existed and has the potential to exist. That is true reality. Here on earth, we define reality as what we can see or feel, or touch, through our senses. But physical bodies on earth are but one dimension, a limited dimension. If you place that single dimension up against everything that's ever existed, you will notice the difference between our perception of what's real and what truly is real.

140

Marissa nodded in understanding. "What was the vacuum of love I experienced?" she asked as I confirmed that the tape recorder was still recording.

By leaving our physical bodies behind, we leave behind earthly trauma and the feelings connected to our earthly senses. Only when we leave behind those emotions, are we truly free to experience that which doesn't weigh us down—infinite creation and understanding—which is equivalent to ecstasy.

"Why did I not want to return to earth?" she asked. "This was the most perfect experience and I didn't want to leave!"

As soon as we leave our physical body behind, we are safe in the palms of the universe. We're completely enveloped in the universal All. Beyond our physical body, we forget our earthly trauma and experience perfect peace and bliss.

"That's beautiful," Marissa said and smiled.

Travel to Strange Realms

Like other NDErs, Marissa told me about her strange dreams and connections with others in an alternate reality that sometimes comes to her at night. Over and over again, NDErs told me, in an embarrassed and bashful way, about the times they were taken to other realms, far away, to meet creatures and beings that were frightening and indecipherable.

This is how Spirit explained it:

As an NDEr, Marissa returned to earth with a different energy knitted into her fabric. Marissa's like a transistor radio now, tuned in simultaneously to two stations, which aren't communicating with each other. In this case, they're using Marissa as the connection. She asked for my help with this and with the realms she is being shown and taken to, but I told her that I knew of no remedy. Others who experience this same distressing phenomenon, may be uncomfortable with this as well, but they recognize what is happening, which seems to relieve some of their anxiety, I told her.

The NDE is the gateway to infinity, a connection to everybody and everything. The experience is so large, it stretches the imagination, even as I became accustomed to hearing the tales, the otherworldly experiences, the shocking changes. This was a realm that on one hand, I was becoming immune to, but at the same time, was causing me to recognize the infinite gap and at the same time, the connection between ourselves, others, and the universe.

Marissa and I both recorded the session. At that point in our conversation, she had other questions about her family, her health, and her adjustment to her NDE. Like others I'd spoken with, Marissa told me she had been abused as a child. Although she was learning forgiveness through her NDE, she wasn't quite there yet. But she was very grateful for the reading, and said it had helped her. She had felt isolated and had many questions, and the reading had provided some answers. Because of her former profession in the media, she knew instinctively what pieces of information might be important to me and to her story. That skill helped to make her process go smoothly.

After the reading, I shut down my laptop, turned out the lights, closed the door behind me, and started out for a walk, to integrate what I'd learned and to clear myself from the reading.

Sound and the Vibration of the Harp

The harp, the instrument Marissa was guided to play, has occupied a place in legend as long as it has been an instrument, perhaps because of its powerful effect, including its ability to transport the listener to an elevated state of consciousness. Present-day orchestral music employs the modern harp to depict the celestial hereafter. It's not surprising that across cultures, the harp shows up as a prominent symbol for the afterlife.

Harps are part of the ancient family of chordophone instruments, instruments in which the sound is made from the vibrations of strings. The harp contains elements of both sound and vibration, and vibration is critical to the production of the harp's sound, key to Marissa's choice of instrument to initiate her mission.

The vibration generated by the harp can reach out and raise consciousness in a unique manner among musical instruments, even from the instruments we examined in Lyla's music (see Chapter 7) and other stringed instruments, with thicker strings that vibrate slower and produce a lower frequency.

Let's examine how the harp works: Marissa's harp sends a signal to the body to create a gentle but powerful vibration, a blissful state. The harp's soothing timbre can produce reverberating sounds that connect with the body through our energetic centers. The harp's large size allows it to produce a unique vibration. It is capable of delivering a sound that unites and connects us all.

Like other NDErs (Lynnclaire [see Chapter 11], Dan [see Chapter 6], and Bob [see Chapter 6]) Marissa's gift relates back to ancient times. The earliest harps and lyres were found in Sumer in 3500 BCE and the origin of the harp to Mesopotamia, like Sacred Geometry, mathematics, and other archaic links to the NDE and its after-effects. The harps origins are ancient, at least to the first millennium.

The harp has been depicted as a powerful manipulator of bodily states, with the purported ability to induce sleep. According to the Druids, the harp was able to traverse the threshold between worlds. Indeed, it is a powerful symbol of the transcendent state of the NDE.

Let's now examine another strange after-effect, which goes beyond our three-dimensional world. Now we come to Mark Jacoby and his unusual electrical ability.

13 ✳ Mark Jacoby and Physiological Transformation: ✳ Electromagnetic Sensitivity

> "If the presence of electricity can be made
> visible in any part of the circuit, I see no
> reason why intelligence may not be
> transmitted instantaneously by electricity."
> —Samuel Morse

I was on a plane looking out over the patchwork of ground below, my third trip that year to Tucson. This time, I was heading to The Science of Consciousness conference at the University of Arizona.

I thought back to my previous visits to Tucson. There was the first NDEr I met, the diver who drowned and spoke at the local chapter meeting of IANDS (International Association for Near- Death Experiencers) several years ago. There was Lyla (see Chapter 7) and then Dan Rhema (see Chapter 6) and his connection to Tucson. The University of Arizona and their work in the field of consciousness.

I thought about the Shaman in Santa Fe and remembered the city I was shown in my journey with the Shaman—the city that was lit up like a marquee. All of a sudden I realized: It was Tucson. A place I had visited again and again. A place where the circle opened and now began to close.

The previous week, Mark Jacoby contacted me. Mark is known as "the man who talks to machines." Yes, this sounds impossible, but Mark's story is true. I reached for a folder from my bag under my seat and looked through my notes about Mark.

Mark had called one evening to say he had been dreaming of me the night before. He knew I would call him, he said, and he wanted to make contact.

Mark Jacoby builds, designs, and operates fiber-optic disk storage networks. Much of what he does is classified. He began his career in the military in electronic counter measures warfare. He worked on the big secret machines that make airplanes invisible. Today, Mark works on the biggest storage networks in the world.

After we chatted about his experience and the research I was doing, Mark and I made arrangements to speak the following Tuesday. I called Mark at our agreed-upon time, and he picked up right away. I heard him rustling papers in the background. "Sorry," he said. "I'm trying to help my son with some stuff."

I took a sip of tea and waited. I looked at Mark on my computer screen, a dark-haired man in his 40s who look harried. Soon, he brushed his hair off his face and began to tell me his story.

Mark's NDE

"I am not trying to convince anybody of anything. I am simply relaying an experience," he explained.

Mark was only 17 when he had his NDE, in which he experienced an incredible trip to the inner workings of the universe.

December 17, 1979, was a snowy day in Lake Tahoe. Mark Jacoby was a 17-year-old senior at Lake Tahoe High when he and a friend decided to listen to the latest Pink Floyd album at his friend's lakefront home. "My friend had a new Jeep and good snow tires, but the snow was coming down hard and fast. The plows couldn't keep up, and the roads quickly turned slick and icy," he said.

Mark and his friend made it safely to the friend's condo and spent the lunch hour talking and listening to music. Meanwhile, the weather turned treacherous and, as they returned to school after lunch, Mark's friend lost control of the car.

"The jeep accelerated and slid completely out of control," Mark said. "We headed for a telephone pole. But, I was thinking we're going to get stuck and have to dig out."

Mark paused, then continued his story: "My friend was ejected across a snow bank and I went out the drivers side; my rib cage bent the steering wheel in half. My last memory was a loud sound, accompanied by a brief flash of light."

When Mark awoke, his whole body was tingling. There was a hissing sound in his ears and he was having trouble breathing. Talking was becoming more difficult. He passed out.

He came to when the highway patrolman arrived and started asking questions. "By this time I couldn't breathe enough to speak above a quiet whisper. I identified myself and said we'd crashed in the jeep, but he couldn't hear me."

Mark was taken to a nearby house and his shirt was cut off.

"I tried to look at my deformed body but began to feel as though I wasn't looking at my body at all. The air seemed fuzzy, like I could see the molecules. My perspective had changed and I was looking down at the paramedics.

"I kept exhaling, like I had been sucked out by some sort of vacuum. I willed myself to turn my vision toward the sofa and saw my body lying on the sofa below me."

Mark was aware that something very strange was happening. The paramedics knew he had stopped breathing.

"I don't believe I knew I was dying yet. But I did know this was serious. When I realized I was not in my body, there was a moment of panic. Then I felt like I was being drawn away, becoming part of something else. The people in the room looked as if their outlines had been traced with a crayon of light. The air became a purple hue, like the molecules were translucent. I could sense the snow falling as I merged upward.

"I knew this place. It was familiar. It felt like home.

"I remember feeling as if a tremendous burden had been lifted from me. I do recall a deep sense of love. Deeper than I had ever experienced. It seemed to emanate from all points and from me outward. And a sense of belonging. This was the most tranquil and peaceful moment in my life."

We paused for a moment and then I asked, "Was a family member with you?"

"I could feel the presence of another. Acceptance and understanding of all my feelings were shared instantly with this being who loved me unconditionally. Then came a voice. I cannot say whether this was God, my spirit guide, Jesus, or some relative. I wasn't concerned with labels and today I see truth in many topics. I can say that this voice and I were together in some profound way."

"Did you have a life review?" I asked.

"The voice asked me many questions at once. 'Are you done with this life? Do you want to finish the work you were to do? Do you want your loved ones to experience this grief?' All of this was asked in an instant. I could feel a great many thoughts, even from people I didn't know, people who read the news or heard it on the radio. Somehow, I could feel all the repercussions of my death at once. I remember thinking about my mom, and parts of my life, all in a flash. My recollection is that the choice was mine. For each version of the question, I felt the feelings and repercussions of my decision."

At that point, Mark digressed. "I need to tell you about my background," he said. "I was adopted as an infant and grew up to be a troublemaker. I hurt other children, had taken to drug and alcohol abuse, got bad grades, was involved in vandalism. All of these actions were relived in a nutshell, with the feelings of myself and the parties involved. But most profound was the sense of how my mother felt to hear of my death. She was in great pain, but it was mixed with feelings of how much trouble I had been. I got a sense that it was such a tragedy to end this life never really having done much good. Somewhere beneath this overwhelming feeling of grief was a sense of duty and work I had to do."

Mission. There it was again—that sense of a purpose. It had surfaced with Lewis (see Chapter 4), Bob (see Chapter 6), Dan (see Chapter 6), Lynnclaire (see Chapter 11), Marissa (see Chapter 12), and others.

Mark was given a choice: stay or go back?

He said, "My response was to pose a question: 'If I go back will I be able to come here later? Will it always be like this?' The answer was immediate. The result instantaneous. There was an oxygen mask on my face and I was struggling to wake up.

"Medical prognosis? I was crushed between a jeep and a telephone pole. I had extensive trauma, bruised ribs, broken bones and hemorrhaging, a possible bruised aorta, and my right lung was punctured."

I realized I had been holding my breath. I exhaled and breathed normally. "What happened next?" I asked.

"The experience changed me profoundly. For years, I didn't discuss it, for fear of ridicule, and because it was so personal. But now, I don't care if anybody believes me."

S trengthened Abilities

Mark returned with several physiological after-effects, the most pronounced being his ability to electronically connect with machines.

Mark said the relationship between himself and the machines began in the hospital, right after his accident: "It happened immediately. I could feel and sense the electromagnetic fields associated with the wires, the remote control, and the machines in the hospital room. I can influence machine operation, sense electronics, and feel electron flow. In the hospital after the accident, I stopped my heart through thought."

"How in the world did you do that?" I asked, imagining lights flashing and alarms being triggered in his hospital room.

"I wish you could have seen the nurse," Mark said. "It was almost like I personally was going into the internals of the machine to learn how the EKG worked. The way to turn off the machine was to stop giving it the signal. So I turned my heart off."

I paused. So, Mark can interrupt current flow like a human circuit breaker? What is this strange electronic capability that Mark possesses?

"I can look at a schematic next to a machine and almost feel what components are broken," he says. "It's a physical sensation."

Ken had also remarked on sensing light and electricity as pressure (see Chapter 10). Other NDErs share electronic sensitivity, although not as extreme a case as Mark.

Mark says his sensitivity and other "phenomena" definitely increase and decrease in cycles, from cosmic influences and earth/sun magnetic fluctuations, all phenomenon that exert a pull on energy.

I asked if Mark was able to turn off his sensitivity with machines at will.

"I am now," he said, "but it took some time before I could keep this field I interact with from interfering with my work and life. It's a bit like dealing with an infant. The same hand that feeds and changes diapers could also snap bones."

I wanted to examine Mark's after-effects more closely. We arranged to converse in a few days. What would Mark's session tell us about his powerful abilities?

Mark's Session

A week later, shortly after 3 p.m., I dialed Mark on Skype. I wondered how the reading would go, given the depth of his NDE.

I heard a loud noise in the background when Mark answered, and it took a second to realize it was the sound of thunder.

"Are you ready?" I asked Mark after a few preliminary adjustments to the sound and volume. He nodded. As I peered at him through the laptop screen, I noted that his aura, like others, was pure white. Spirit was protecting him. Here's what came through me:

Your aura is extremely bright, filled with white light, like looking at a million-watt bulb right in my face. It's the light of the universe.

Mark was most curious about his after-effects, asking, "How did my after-effects get turned on in my NDE?"

Here's what Spirit showed me: Mark's NDE and after-effects blossomed alongside Mark when he returned. I was shown symbols for electron flow and enhancement that became more complex and substantial following his NDE. As Mark gave birth to his NDE on earth, it became a living thing.

I watched Mark out of the corner of my eye and noted that he was listening. "Are you okay?" I asked, wondering what he thought about the reading.

"Yes," he said.

"How do we explain what happened to Mark in his NDE?" we asked.

Mark is like a sophisticated circuit board or antennae programmed to a unique channel. His antennae is capable of tuning in to other frequencies, and granting him extraordinary access into all aspects of the universe. His energy is universal and transcends our earth plane.

Astrophysics confirms that our universe is filled with energy. Radio bursts from outer space are reported as high-energy cosmic rays that have an impact on the earth's atmosphere. Mark, in essence, is able to communicate with these high-energy rays.

Mark inhabits a difficult space. I shivered as I contemplated all the NDErs I met who occupied this space as well. In Mark's reading, I was taken to this faraway realm. And in his reading, I would go farther into this realm than in other readings and relay this information to him.

Mark has crisscrossed space and the universe. He is extremely complex, a universal body of multi-dimensional energy, which exists in an elevated realm of infinite time and space.

I was shown a tableau of time and the universe, combined with other concepts of the universe that represented Mark's gifts.

What does Mark have to say about this? What is it like to live with this capability?

He drained his glass of water before answering me. "I'm pretty isolated in this most of the time," he said.

I went "offline" to let him know that most NDErs seem to share that sense of isolation. Then I picked up again.

"How is Mark able to communicate with machines?" we asked.

Mark's entire body is a highly developed, sensing component programmed to a frequency, and calibrated to a non-earth based channel.

Mark is actually a cyber-intuitive. He returned from his NDE with powerful electronic gifts, gifts that our system is not equipped to deal with. While the rest of us have to manually flick on a light switch to turn on the lights in a room, Mark is like a human/cyborg. There is no system on earth to accommodate him in his double existence.

Like other NDErs, Mark was struggling, so I asked, "Why Mark? What was there about Mark that marked him as a candidate?"

I was shown a car going along a road full of ruts. Not making any progress. Just getting into another rut. Then Spirit said:

Mark was identified as raw material, if we could just reconfigure him. Straighten him out for other options and possibilities, so that he would evolve.

Mark wanted to know about the sense of love he experienced: the what or who that emanated from All? "What was that?" he asked.

It was the All that encompasses everything. All the planets, all the constellations, all the stars. All of us. All of the universes and everything that reaches beyond infinity. Then double or triple that.

Mark also asked about the presence of another during his NDE. "Who or what was that?"

When Mark met the Other—the Other he felt he already knew—that information was already embedded and existed, within him. Mark had already met everybody, knew everything, before that moment. Mark possessed a little slice of everything that ever existed, that's ever been thought of, within his consciousness. Mark never had the opportunity to be face-to-face with anything beyond his earthly container before that moment. Yet, during his NDE, Mark was able to tap into universal consciousness. For Mark, it was like meeting a part of himself that was there all along.

Many NDErs say they are given information in their journey yet don't remember all of it when they return. Mark felt as if he was shown the universe and was exposed to great knowledge, like Marissa and Ken and Lynnclaire, yet he doesn't remember it all.

"Mark could only return with a portion of that knowledge. As it was, he was returning to a physical body with a great deal of trauma. There was a limit to what he could manage. The universe only gave him what he could return with."

I watched Mark smile before he continued. "What caused the hissing sound I heard as I floated through the ceiling?" he asked.

Your consciousness was sliding out of your body, exiting into another realm. This is not a sound we are accustomed to on earth, yet we call it a hiss or a buzz.

Mark frowned. "I was able to see and feel atoms in the air during my NDE. How was this possible?"

Your consciousness is permeable. It went up right against those atoms and molecules and was able to understand and recognize them as a form of matter unrecognizable to us. In that state, you were able to be at one with the smallest units of the universe.

Mark is able to turn off his electrical sensitivity now but says it took years to keep the field he interacts with from interfering with his work and life.

Mark and I chatted for several more minutes about the reading, and then he shook his head and said, "You get so close," remarking on what I had seen in his session.

So close, I repeated to myself silently. Then I added, "It's not me," I said. "I am just the facilitator. I am shown what Spirit wants me to see and then I pass it on to you."

I am just a channel, someone used to transmit information. The information generally does not "stick" to me. It passes through and I listen carefully, so that I am able to pass it on, to the best of my ability, to the sitter, the person I am reading for. I bring in the energy and search for the answers and then relay them. That is all I do.

Mark's reading was a bit different, because I felt and saw how he had spent much of his experience "out there." It made his reading more complex and added information about the Cosmos and the universe, that were not as present in other readings.

Did Mark go farther than others? He certainly had a complicated experience and I was taken there with him. All that happened to Mark was deep, too vast for us to understand it all.

Electromagnetic Sensitivity

Electrical matter consists of particles extremely subtle, since it can permeate common matter, even the densest metals, with such ease and freedom as not to receive any perceptible resistance.

—Benjamin Franklin

I paged through my records, noting the frequency of electrical sensitivity. I noted the man who broke the ticket machine at the movies, the woman who caused the ATM to malfunction, and the person who busted the parking garage arm. I thought about Mark's after-effects and the components of energy—at least what I knew about energy. We are all energetic beings. We all have frequencies.

It is now widely accepted by scientists that electromagnetic interactions are fundamental to the workings of biological tissue. We are all energetic beings with frequencies that govern our activities, and on earth, we operate at low electrical frequencies. Yet, NDErs appear to return with a unique, higher-frequency energy—an energy that not only interferes with ordinary stationary equipment but collaborates with a higher plane. We don't know what this energy is but we know it interacts with our electromagnetic field.

This energy is from realms that are not linear, planes very far away from our three-dimensional world. We are part of a much vaster whole we cannot even contemplate. Currently, even scientists don't understand or possess a conceptual framework for understanding this energy. This energetic realm is so far beyond us in evolution and functioning that it eludes our conventional explanations.

Mark's electrical after-effects are specific. However, many NDErs experience electrical after-effects: street lights that turn off when they pass, computers that malfunction, glitches in cell phones and appliances. NDEs are electrically charged events, and many NDErs conduct electricity at a much higher frequency post-NDE.

To date, research into electrical sensitivity in NDErs has been limited. One researcher, Jan Holden at the University of Texas, has facilitated studies into electrical sensitivity. Her research suggests that electronic sensitivity is linked to the depth of the NDE, as measured by the Greyson scale. (See Appendix A.)

The issue with this hypothesis is that many people who've never experienced an NDE are also electrically sensitive. Others who don't remember their NDEs are also electrically sensitive. And some with high scores on the Greyson scale have no electrical sensitivity at all. This suggests that electrical sensitivity is not tied to a scale but rather to encounters with noetic experiences, and electrical events, including anything from meditation to cardiac arrests to lightning strikes.

Once we understand the energetic realm that NDErs journey to, that NDErs like Mark Jacoby return with electrical sensitivity, large or small, should be of no surprise. I have seen a smattering of it—glimpses of these strange universes and realms so unlike our earth, it makes our world look limited by comparison.

I stopped and looked up as the pilot announced that we would land in Tucson soon. In the dim light I glanced at my watch and closed my folder of notes on Mark Jacoby. Two hours had passed, and the mystery of the NDE was still illusory as I watched the sun set over the Catalina Mountains.

14 ✳ *Mary Ann Mernaugh and Cognitive Transformation:* ✳ *Enhanced IQ*

"Our mind is capable of passing beyond
the dividing line we have drawn for it."

—Hermann Hesse

I clicked through my emails and noticed one that said, "Please contact me. I experienced an increased IQ through my NDE years ago." It was signed "Mary Ann Mernaugh, Laguna Beach, California."

I replied to Mary Ann and, by the following day, I heard back from her.

Mary Ann was one of many people I'd met whose lives had been turned upside-down after her NDE. Her experience took her on a completely new path, influencing her relationships, her career, her mission, and all her beliefs.

Mary Ann's near-death experience occurred in 1969, before 13 million Americans admitted they shared this supernatural experience, and before the term *NDE* was coined by Raymond Moody. The press and Hollywood media had yet to seize on the idea of a near-death experience, to glamorize it as an arresting and entertaining spectacle to enthrall their audiences.

Mary Ann said:

"I was 26 at the time of my NDE and in labor with my first child. As I lay on the delivery table, I began to rapidly go down a tunnel. I remember thinking, *Oh my God! I'm dying.*

"I saw a bright light in the distance and then everything went black. When I woke up, I thought I was dead and in heaven. I felt wonderful. Peaceful and warm. Someone walked in the room and my bubble broke. I knew I was alive."

Mary Ann's NDE was as real as any experience she has ever had—more so, she says. As she recalls, there was nothing dreamlike about it,

154

and it continues to be a highly acute memory with details especially memorable—a complete sensory experience. In addition, she says, "It completely defies comparison in the human experience and is permanently imprinted on my conscious mind."

Mary Ann's near-death experience was brief but she shares the aspect of electrical sensitivity with others:

"I had difficulty with electrical appliances. I could never get the copy machine at work to function properly. It would do all kinds of crazy things like change its settings and refuse to print. I could scramble the numbers on hand held calculators, too."

Mary Ann was uncertain what happened to her that day in the hospital, but her family was touched by the tragedy of her newborn dying only nine hours after birth.

"I had no knowledge at the time what a near-death experience was. I didn't have the foggiest of what happened and I couldn't put a label on it.

"Stupidly, I went to church and told the priest in confessional that I was really hurting. I didn't understand why this was happening to me. He told me that I deserved to have my child die because I had used birth control.

"I didn't understand that I had an NDE until seven years later when I read a news supplement in the Sunday paper and saw a picture of what is today known as the tunnel."

Mary Ann didn't talk about her experience to anyone until she met a woman who encouraged her to speak about it. This was long after she made several life changes that she now knows were a result of her NDE.

"I had the strong feeling after my NDE, that everyone has a path, a vocation, a mission," she said. "Whatever you choose to call it. I had to find that mission on my own."

After her NDE, Mary Ann knew she had to change her life. She had no money, her father had recently passed away, and she was in a difficult marriage.

Mary Ann's Transformation

Prior to her NDE, Mary Ann attended Michigan Tech University. "As an undergraduate, the University did thorough testing on all its freshman. My IQ was measured at 123 at that point," she says. Mary Ann's IQ registered in the above-average range.

But, after her NDE, Mary Ann began to notice dramatic changes to her mental process.

She noticed she was thinking in a different way. Things seemed crisper and clearer, her thought process more acute. She could compile figures in her head faster after her NDE than she could before her experience. Mary Ann recalls specific examples, including this one: "My family and I were watching figure skating on TV and it was being judged on a 10-point system with fractions. The judges compiled, then averaged, the figures. I was able to compile and average the figures before the final total was posted on TV. I was driving my niece crazy. She kept asking me how I was doing it.

"I was able to fly through complex IQ tests. While in graduate school, I had to take a class in psychometrics. One of the exercises involved giving mental acuity test questions to a partner until the partner missed two questions. My partner finally called the instructor over and said, 'I can't get her to miss two questions. We just keep going.' The instructor told us to just stop and mark the end point. Ironically, I also scored high on the Pons test, which measures the ability to read non-verbals—face, body, and voice cues."

Mary Ann had tangible evidence that her IQ increased after her NDE—that her cognitive processes changed. She also had her IQ tested by the local Mensa organization and scored 145 on the California Mental Maturity test, which put her in the top 1 percent of the population. Overall, her IQ increased 22 points after her NDE.

Mary Ann went on to earn two master's degrees with 4.0 GPAs and honors. After her first master's degree, she worked for 12 years in microbiology, and eventually completed one year of internship and two years of residency to become a clinical therapist.

How do we explain Mary Ann's enhanced intelligence? What occurred to deliver Mary Ann's new powers?

Mary Ann's Session

Mary Ann and I agreed to Skype the following week. She was eager to be involved with the work. She believed, similar to Mark (see Chapter 13) and Marissa (see Chapter 12), that she was shown many things about the universe in her NDE, but because she couldn't remember all of them, she was especially interested in a reading. "Things have been slow, so this will be great!" she said.

Then I got an email letting me know that Mary Ann was having surgery. The session was off. I was disappointed but also concerned about Mary Ann.

Mary Ann contacted me a few months later. With the surgery behind her, she was fine and ready to go forward, adding, "I'll never say that things are slow again!"

A week later, I checked the time: almost 4:00—1:00 West Coast time. I ran a comb through my hair and placed a few crystals next to the computer. I took a seat at the kitchen table and called Mary Ann. She was already online waiting. When she answered, I leaned in and moved closer to the screen.

Mary Ann looked as I imagined she would: shoulder-length blond hair, a fresh-faced woman with the healthy, attractive, all-American, "Doris Day" look.

I quieted myself and breathed in the scent of the sandalwood incense that I had burned earlier in the day. I felt the tension flow out of my body as I grounded myself. I looked up and asked Mary Ann if she was ready.

She nodded and began with a comment to me: "I always felt that a lot more happened in my NDE but my memory was blocked. Isn't that strange? I've tried over the years to find out what else it was, but I was never able to." She was eager to find out why she didn't remember more and grateful to have the opportunity to explore this question in a reading.

Not so strange, we learned. It's as if these individuals are embedded with the knowledge of the universe, regardless of their active memories. The NDErs may not be able to access all the information when they return to earth, yet the events exist permanently, recorded in their consciousness.

Similar to other NDErs, Mary Ann couldn't take all the information back with her because it would simply be too burdensome once she resumed her earth life. Just having the experience was more than enough. Can you imagine if you nearly died, saw a light brighter than a billion suns, met deceased relatives, had life lessons, and then were shown the secrets to the universe? What would you do? Maybe you wouldn't want any more "gifts" to remember?

As with Mark and others who received information from the universe, the knowledge is carefully parceled out by Spirit. Spirit only gives us what we can handle, whether in an NDE, in our daily lives, or in parts of our journeys. Even though NDErs can process everything in the unseen realm of the NDE, they can't handle it all when they return home.

I settled in, took a deep breath, and felt my skin tingling. I listened as Mary Ann asked the first question. "What happened in my NDE to transform my life?" she wondered.

Mary Ann was infused with the light. There's nothing stronger than the power of the light—a magnet that redirects and rearranges all it encounters. Once it's implanted in an individual, they're never the same. Something from outside the physical now prods them, as if a switch has been turned on. And remains on.

Like other NDErs, Mary Ann was on a course to uncover her mission. As a result of her remarkable after-effects, Mary Ann discovered her life calling. Yet, Mary Ann doesn't remember making a pact with the universe. She had the sense there was profound order, and that the experience affected her mind, her power, when she returned, and her ability to understand many things. But she couldn't remember a deal, a transaction, an arrangement.

Having a near-death experience and all its after-effects is disconcerting and disorienting. All the experiencers ask the same question: What are you supposed to do with it? Because no matter what you get, it doesn't adapt to the system we live by on earth.

According to Mary Ann, some people have NDEs to show them they must change their life. "Some, like me, have experiences to give them ammunition to help them make quantum changes," she said. "I believe there is a spiritual reason," she added.

Mary Ann had additional personal questions about the next phase of her life, and we spent some time chatting and exploring them. After we finished, after being in the realm of Spirit, I needed to experience the earth, nature, trees, and the sky. As I do after many readings, I threw on my sneakers and left the house, to head to the park. Walking grounds me after a reading and allows me to clear myself to resume my life.

IQ and the NDE

What was it about the higher intelligence that Mary Ann acquired? How was she able to achieve a 22-point increase in IQ? If the answer couldn't be found in our session, perhaps research could provide additional clues?

I began by looking into the drivers of IQ. IQ itself is difficult to define, although, put simply, it's our ability to reason and understand and a measure of our cognitive abilities. IQ labels have changed since the beginning of IQ testing, but tests are generally reliable enough that you have similar scores throughout your life. Yet, unlike most of us, Mary Ann's scores did not remain constant. Following her NDE, Mary Ann's scores went from above average to the upper extreme of intelligence, the very gifted range.

I thought about what I knew about brain enhancement and the factors that would impact intelligence as I began to probe Mary Ann's exceptional after-effect. I turned up information on smart drugs, supplements, cognitive enhancers, and genetic markers. None of these were the answer. What happened to Mary Ann didn't involve pharmaceuticals, and besides, her experience happened before the introduction of recently developed drugs. There was no evidence that her genetic makeup was the answer either, as the growth in her IQ was gradual.

If it wasn't drugs, enhancers, supplements, or genes, what affected Mary Ann's IQ?

I decided to look into binaural beats—sounds caused by specific stimulation. I had already looked at their role as enhancers of consciousness and suspected they were not the answer to Mary Ann's question. Binaural beats result when the brain integrates two separate signals and interprets the third signal, the sound produced, as a binaural beat. The frequency of binaural beats, the Hz achieved, are not high enough to induce higher intelligence. I also discarded the effects of age and environment. It's generally acknowledged that IQ declines with age and that no environmental factor has a strong influence on IQ after the critical mid-teen years.

I knew from previous work that Mary Ann entered a different energetic space. She, just as others did, had taken the express elevator to the highest realms of consciousness. So I decided to look into higher energetic realms, so to speak.

Brain Waves and Frequency

The brain, made up of billions of cells called neurons, is an electrochemical organ capable of generating as much as 10 watts of electrical power. These neurons are worker bees and use electricity to communicate with each other. This combined electrical activity is described as brain waves. The nerve cells that fire electrical signals are called brainwave patterns.

As are other frequencies in your body, brain waves are measured in hertz (Hz), and these electrical signals are affected by vibrations that enter our body. The role and function of brain waves and electrical activity emanating from the brain seemed a path worth investigating. Besides, as I thought about sound and light waves and their impact on Ken's and Robert's enhanced abilities (see Chapter 10), it seemed that waves and frequencies were related to NDE after-effects.

New frequencies that stimulate our body's mental functions have recently been discovered. I resolved to look into the therapeutic aspects of subtle energy fields to learn more and see if there was a link between energy fields and intelligence.

Gamma brain waves, the highest frequency brain wave, or the elite of brain waves, are linked to intellectual properties and executive functions such as higher IQ. Up until recently, gamma waves have received little attention from researchers. Gamma waves, at a frequency of 40–70 Hz, are the fastest and smallest brainwaves and allow parts of the brain to communicate with each other. According to a study published in *Nature Neuroscience*, applying electrical current to the brain shows that inducing brain waves of a specific frequency produces the electrical activity of gamma waves.[1]

Studies have demonstrated that brainwave patterns can be altered through a variety of stimuli, including sound and light. Stimulation of the brain produces alterations, and, at a very high frequency, may produce what we regard as "gifts" (higher abilities, higher IQ). Can gamma waves be altered through an NDE? Can gamma waves, associated with information processing, cognition and consciousness, be affected by a noetic experience?

According to recent research at the University of Michigan and published in the *Proceedings of the National Academy of Sciences*, high levels of brainwave activity have been found at the moment of death in laboratory rats.[2] If a sharp increase in high-frequency brainwaves, called gamma oscillations, are present at or near death, would this explain the underpinnings of Mary Ann's higher IQ?

The frequency signature of the NDE—the frequency that remains with the experiencer—conveys multiple properties: to heal, to grow; to learn better, to think better, to stimulate creativity. It appears as if Mary Ann was exposed to a frequency that increased her capability of processing information and higher functions. Is it possible she encountered a frequency that interacted with her brain's gamma waves to increase her intelligence?

Or does this increased intelligence go beyond the brain and brain waves? Perhaps an X factor from the universe?

We have no way to be certain as we search this baffling puzzle on the border of science and spirituality where so much remains unknown.

15 ✳ Ana Callan and Cognitive Transformation: ✳ Poetry and Verse

> "Poetry is as exact a science as geometry."
>
> —Gustave Flaubert

As I paged through *The Baltimore Sun*, the light streamed through the slatted blinds in my office. My cell phone chirped—a text from my old friend Rich, a friend from my days in the investment business. I hadn't seen him in years, but he reminded me of a time long past.

"I thought of you today since it was the 10-year anniversary of Google going public. Do you ever get to NY?" he texted.

"Sure," I texted back. "I'm up there about once a month."

In spite of the work I was doing, I tried to get to New York for art events and the opera, or to visit friends when I could.

Rich and I agreed to meet for dinner on my next trip, so we could catch up with each other's lives, settling on Balthazar, a bistro in Lower Manhattan.

Two weeks later on a mild weekday evening, I strolled down Spring Street, taking in the boutiques, the artists' lofts, and the cast-iron buildings. When I entered the restaurant, I spied Rich at the bar, drinking champagne. He waved me over.

As I sat down, Rich filled me in on his business. Sounding wistful, he said, "Clients are dying [he meant it literally; his clients were older], the business has become a commodity. Things have really changed."

When Rich asked what I was up to, I smiled and said, "You might want to have a drink." I went on to explain that I was a psychic now and told him about the work I was doing with NDEs.

A long patch of silence followed. He didn't alter the blank expression on his face. He didn't utter a sound or ask a question. Just silence.

I filled in a few more details and then he said, "I thought it was a good idea to get together since it was the 10-year anniversary of Google going public."

That was it, the extent of his response.

I don't know what he was thinking, but I didn't think it was good. I've learned that the reactions to this work and my shift from the traditional path in the investment business, to work that many don't take seriously, are all part of my journey. I've experienced the cold shoulder, and been challenged, pooh-poohed, and tested. As my father used to say, "You've got to play the hand that's dealt you."

Two years earlier I might have had another reaction to Rich—maybe tried to shift the conversation back to the mantle I wore as a business-woman and investor. Instead, I just said, "Rich, I just explained to you what I was doing and you didn't react."

"If you think you can do this, I'm happy for you," he said.

I knew better than to press it.

I'll admit not everyone is supportive of this work. I've made peace with the fact that I'm doing something outside the mainstream. I might just have more company as the years go by; I'd have to wait to see. The years of being on the frontier in the investment business, taught me that it can be lonely work. And now I was on the frontier yet again, doing different work.

After three years of research, I had begun to look at death, the after-life, and the NDE differently. When I started this work, I told various people—my family, a few friends—about what I was doing, but I didn't tell everyone. I wasn't sure what kind of reaction I'd get, and didn't want to have to explain myself or the fact that I'm a psychic.

I wasn't worried about what my family thought, even from the beginning. My boys were always supportive; they asked questions and sent me articles about the after-life and near-death experiences. As time went on, I found some folks had no judgment and were truly interested, whereas others were skeptical and thought I was "off." I shrugged any negativity off. As I adapted, I even began to think of myself as "normal."

As I worked with the experiencers, I learned from each encounter. These people had special gifts, and some were in a position to share them with others. And the work wasn't just about the after-effects any more. It hadn't been for a long time. It was about a million other things.

By that time, several people asked me if poetry was an after-effect of NDEs, and I knew that it was. I had spoken to several poets who told me about flashes of verse that would come to them in one full flush, without revision, in their dreams or even during the workday. One was an NPR host, another a man who had written an autobiographical theater piece about his experience, and another a tech industry exec who is awakened in the middle of the night as streams of poetry enter his consciousness.

Ana's Poetry After-Effect

Ana Callan received poetry as an NDE after-effect. Her NDE occurred in Dublin, Ireland, after a near-fatal accident when she was 41. When she recounts her NDE, Ana explains that she saw that everything in life happened in what she called "utter perfection—seamless, exquisite, and whole."

Immediately after her accident, Ana couldn't write and had difficulty expressing herself. She began to play with words in her head and soon began to see the hidden meaning behind letters and phrases. As she put it, it was like "cracking a secret code. It gave me a sense of being connected to something much larger than myself."

Ana later discovered that poetry was the only vehicle that could express her experience, because poetry distills the experience down to the essentials. Since her NDE, Ana also experienced a growing communion with animals and birds, like Ken (see Chapter 10), and she was puzzled by that.

When Ana and I connected, she mentioned the timing was fortuitous because the next day was the 14th anniversary of her NDE. She was just beginning to explore her experience further.

As we chatted, it soon became clear that Ana and I shared other links. We traded a few stories, and found that she lived in Baltimore and attended Johns Hopkins University, where I had taught. She herself taught at the Hopkins Center for Talented Youth, which my children attended. I took these synchronicities as a sign that I was on the right path.

Ana was teaching at the University of Dublin when she had her NDE. She was walking along a footpath when a truck loaded with lumber flew over a bump. Ana was struck by the flying lumber, which was flung loose.

Within moments, she was thrown out of her body. As she looked down on the pavement, she saw a broken woman, blood, and curious onlookers, gawking at the tragedy. She couldn't understand why everyone was so upset and had no identification with the woman on the ground.

There was a magnetic pull into the love and light immediately, she said. First, Ana encountered a series of caves, ominous and dark, filled with other beings. Ana recognized these beings and communicated to them: "I told them I was going to be gone for a very long time and implored them to take over for me. I received a very, very strong message that nobody was willing to do that. That I had to come back. There was incredible resistance, then I was back in my body and in the ambulance."

As she lay in the ambulance and went in and out of consciousness, Ana realized, *"Oh my God! It's me!"*

After the accident, Ana didn't want to be here anymore. The blow to her head was a challenge, and her body was broken and crushed. She couldn't stand or sit for long due to the pain, and her mental faculties were impaired. "I would try to say the word *lilac* and the word *lettuce* would come out," she said.

Before her accident, Ana earned her MFA at Johns Hopkins and wrote non fiction essays and a novel. But after her NDE, poetry was the only vehicle that could describe her experience.

"Poetry was the only thing that kept me going," Ana said. "It saved my life."

At first, Ana could only hold one line of poetry at a time in her head. She would take that one line and repeat it over and over.

"It is almost impossible to be here," she would repeat.

The kind of poetry Ana began to write after her NDE took on a much more mystical tone than her earlier work. At first, her poems were devotional, to God or the higher self. Later, another kind of poetry emerged: poetry infused with love and encouragement, pointing toward the deeper truth. Poetry that came through the silence.

"Poems would pour out all day and all night—hundreds and thousands of poems," she said. "I know to the depths of my being that it's not me that's coming through. The poetry is similar to a more authoritative but loving voice, the dissolution of the ego. Completely opposite the type of poetry I wrote prior to the accident, which were personal or about nature."

As Ana says, her poetry seemed linked to a higher authority, a voice that was not individual. A higher power.

Ana's poetry comes in one full flush. She never revises. In addition, others say they come to a state of really deep accord and bliss when Ana shares her poetry. According to Ana, the poetry seems to engender a sense of great peace and connection to those who hear it. She feels as if she's been brought back to live as the Light connected to both the divine and human realms.

Ana believes she is completely transformed since her NDE. She is free of her personal baggage, that denser sense of feeling. She herself seems ultra-light and ethereal in her composure and ease.

Following her NDE, Ana went to Tallahassee to work with the terminally ill and later to Florida State University, where she presented poetry classes to the faculty. "It feels like the whole accident was perfectly orchestrated, and the experience was given to me to heal the cycle of abuse. [Ana experienced abuse as a child.] I left the world for seven years and it was my long dark night," she says about the years following her NDE. She believes she is now being pushed to give back what she received. This is Ana's mission.

Ana now lives in Mt. Shasta, an energetic center in Northern California. As a matter of fact, many NDErs decide to reside in similar energetic centers—Tucson, Mt. Shasta, Louisville, Taos. We would explore the significance of that in her session.

Ana and I agreed to meet on Skype the following week to follow up on her experience.

Ana's Session

The next week I tried to sign on to my computer to connect with Ana but the internet signal was down. I tried again and again. Nothing. Finally I called Ana. We would have to try again later.

Several weeks passed before we reconnected, because Ana was going to a spiritual retreat of silence and I would be traveling.

Ana and I finally Skyped on a warm August evening. Ana was very clear about what she was seeking in the reading. Even though she was receiving her own messages, she was interested in clarity about her work and personal life. I relaxed and breathed deeply and began the reading by noting Ana's aura:

Both of your auras—your physical and spiritual auras—are struggling to heal. While NDE spiritual auras sometimes supersede the physical aura, your spiritual aura is still attempting to rebuild.

This was the first time I had seen a spiritual aura that was still mending, even years after the NDE.

I also noted Ana's third eye, our invisible eye that provides perception beyond ordinary reality. Here's what I saw:

Your third eye chakra is totally open. It shows me the inside of Mt. Shasta, as if you're connected with the source inside that mountain to your core.

We moved on to Ana's NDE, asking: "Why did she have this experience?"

Other experiencers, like Ana, have the "vehicle," the apparatus to go forth and disperse the message of the NDE, but their "power" needs to be adapted to the work. [Unfortunately, NDErs don't come back with an adaptor or converter to convert their powers like foreign travelers use for a different configuration from their 'home' country. They must adapt on their own.] *Some return with powers that lend themselves to our planet. Ana had the tools of her poetic craft already embedded in her, but this ability and her tools would be used differently after her activation from her NDE.*

Like other NDErs, such as Ken, Marissa (see Chapter 12), and Bob (see Chapter 6), Ana's skills—the basics for her missionary work—were already on-board. They were amplified through the NDE and deepened to serve others.

"Was I given a mission during my NDE?"Ana asked.

That mission question. It was always uppermost in the experiencer's minds. I looked up at Ana to see her watching me as the answer came through me.

You weren't told: "Here's your mission." They knew who you were and what you would do when you returned. They knew what your capabilities were. They knew you were a candidate.

Ana asked, "What about timing? Was there something going on in my life that I needed to have an NDE at that time?"

From an emotional viewpoint, your NDE could have happened sooner. It could have interrupted your life—a life of trauma—much earlier. But from a real world point-of-view, it happened later, when you were mature enough to "handle it." Your growth and maturity were far enough along that you could be given the NDE with the expectation that the intended results would occur. In a sense, timing was a factor. Everything converged and there was a readiness.

She nodded. "Yes, that's how it feels," she agreed. "Was there anything in my upbringing or biology that triggered my NDE?" Like others, Ana had suffered abuse as a child and had told me about numerous beatings.

As a child, Ana was not protected. She was ready for something better— ready for the light. Ready for that godly light to be held in divinity. People who go through dark periods are candidates to be held in the hands of divinity.

Ana sat back and considered that, and then her face dawned with recognition. "That's beautiful!" she said.

Ana went on to ask why birds and animals come to her more frequently now. Her experience with the birds and animals was similar to Ken's rapport. I also realized that Shamans use helping spirits in the form of animals and birds to access their spiritual power and wondered if there was a connection between the spirit animals and Ken's and Anna's connections? Between Ken and Ana, I was learning new things about the natural world.

You're attuned to a very high frequency now—the frequency that birds and animals interact with. They recognize it. They listen and are tuned into your same vibration. You are at one with the natural world.

"Well that's beautiful and that makes sense," Ana said.

The Sensing Experience of Consciousness

Ana was concerned about the seamlessness of her connections with others following her NDE. She is physically able to feel and sense what is happening with others, feeling both acute joy and gut-wrenching sorrow almost as if there isn't any separation between herself and others. Life can be complicated enough on its own terms but things get even stickier for Ana.

"Why do I feel what's happening with others?" Ana asked. "I feel it physically, emotionally, mentally, and spiritually."

I told her that since her NDE, she has a chunk of the universe within her. She's merged with the universe and is no longer a single person. She is part of everything that exists, in a sense. "When you've got that chunk within you," I said, "of course you are going to feel what everyone else feels because you're now connected with everyone—and everything."

"Yes, it's so true," she agreed.

Ana also talked about something that frequently happens to her: "When I close my eyes, especially at night or when meditating, I see a constant stream of people. Not just faces but entire bodies. They're indescribably vivid and very close and are often doing different things. Their expressions are palpable. There's no fear about it but I've wondered who they are. It's like being in a packed train and watching everyone up close as they do whatever it is they're doing."

I explained that other NDErs relate similar events. They close their eyes and see stars, unidentifiable people, entities. Sometimes darker images.

When we go to sleep, we depart into the complete unknown. For NDErs, it's more extreme. The people Ana sees when she closes her eyes are there, waiting. Once she's left our plane, she finds herself with everyone who has ever passed and encounters everything—and everyone—that we don't recognize in our waking lives. When we're in our earthly bodies, those people, those beings, are behind the curtain, at bay. Our physical body and its density prevent our consciousness from showing us that reality; it blocks that other realm. But when you go to sleep, the curtain opens. The beings were there all along, but Ana only encounters them then.

The Impact of Energetic Vortexes

"Does being in Mt. Shasta influence the creative?" we wondered. I looked up and, in my computer screen, I spotted Mt. Shasta beyond Ana's window in her study. The white mountain dominates the landscape and has always been the subject of curiosity.

In a place like Mt. Shasta, there's an energetic force, a magnet, that's emitted from the mountain. It's almost like a battery that turns on one's capabilities. And you're right there, too, so you're plugged in to it. There is an attraction that brings you and others there. It's truly a magnetic pull.

The room suddenly felt swelteringly hot. I sat up, took a drink of water and exhaled. I thought about the concept of a magnet, something that had come up before and that I'd explore again. (See Chapter 13.)

Now it was Ana's turn to ask: "Are you okay?"

I sat back and considered my response. Was it Mt. Shasta? Had the mountain also affected me? As someone who operates at a high frequency, conducting a high-frequency event like a reading, I need to be careful not to go too far or too deep.

I spoke slowly. "Yes. I'm fine."

Ana had a few more questions about her personal life and career, and the new poetry book she had finished, and we explored these before we ended the session. She was very methodical in working through the questions, and the session went smoothly and moved along at a good pace.

Within a half hour, the reading was over, and Ana and I said goodbye. I clasped and unclasped my fingers, and arched my back to stretch out the kinks. I was ready for a cold drink and a granola bar to recenter myself.

The Link Between Poetry and the NDE

What about the after-effect of Ana's poetry? Why would poetry be an NDE after-effect? How was poetry linked to other NDE after-effects?

Poetry and spirituality have long literary and cultural links. Ancient Shamans used poetry to maintain a connection between humans and multidimensional beings. Some poets believed that the use of poetry was a path for reaching God and to be of higher service.

Going back centuries, people have depicted their inner and outer worlds through hundreds or thousands of poetic forms. Verse is a form of accounting for a mystical event, a means to explain higher levels of consciousness. Certainly Ana uses it this way. The tales of the Iliad and the Odyssey are long-form epic poems that translate spiritual journeys that have been read and reread for centuries.

Poet mystics have spanned the ages. Visionaries such as Hildegard von Bingen, Mirabai, and Omar Khayyam gave meaning to the universe, to the times and lives of their listeners, moving them to inspiration and adding purpose to their lives. Some poets believe the use of poetry allows their listeners a glimpse of higher worlds, a way to experience what in some cases, only they, as poets, experience.

What was it about Ana's poetry that made it compelling, and how was it linked to her NDE?

Ana's poems are embodied consciousness, which link back to the Universal All. Her poems become a way to describe her journey in her NDE, like Bob's and Dan's art (see Chapter 6), and Marissa's and Lyla's music (see Chapter 7). Ana's poetry functions as a tool to engage readers in a higher dimension. Her combination of words unlocks perceptions deeper than the conscious mind. Ana's poetry, which appears to be mainly channeled, is a way for all of us to connect to the higher state that Ana achieved.

As an ancient form of expression and communication, poetry elicits thoughts and emotions while forging a connection to another place. There is a ritual and a sacredness in Ana's attempts to put her words together to convey meaning, experience, and insight in the listener. With words, Ana's poetry connects our minds with others; it connects us to different moments and places, to transcend the limitations of time and space.

We have seen patterns in many of the NDE after-effects. Poetry also possesses rich patterns, including resonance, rhythm, melody, harmony, and vibration. Some poetry like Ana's also possesses trance-like rhythms that enable the listeners to shift to a higher state.

In poetry, sound is arranged into patterns: the patterns of language, expression, and voice. Pattern and repetition are useful as mechanisms to trigger trance and hypnotic states, as we learned in Lyla's music. Ana seems to have induced a state of trance in herself by repeating over and over "It's almost impossible to be here" following her NDE. Some believe that the patterns of rhythms and tone form the basis for the universe—that patterns make up much of our unseen existence.

The Big Picture: The Universe Entwined in Our Experiences

PART V

16 ✳ Manifestation and Intent: ✳ How Do They Influence NDEs?

"The wound is the place where the
Light enters you."
—Rumi

In north Baltimore, winter turned to spring and, finally, to early summer. As I strolled through Sherwood Gardens, the most famous tulip garden in North America, taking in the yellowish blossoms of the dogwoods, the climbing wisteria, and the pink and purple magnolia blooms, I considered how far I'd come.

As I examined the relationship between the NDE and its after-effects over the years, patterns had developed. The work had been transformed into a correlational experiment of sorts. As you've read and based on what I'd heard from the individuals I interviewed, there seems to be a positive relationship between a type of upbringing and the tendency for an NDE. And the chance of having an NDE also seems to be correlated to certain types of behavior later in life.

I thought about who might be a candidate for this event. It seemed as if these men and women I'd come to know were perpetually out of step. Often alienated, sometimes stuck in ruts or spinning their wheels. They'd had difficult childhoods and had been abused. These profiles would surface again and again. Were there certain psychological or physical parameters that helped explain the NDE? What were the correlates? Was timing a factor? And what role does intent play? I was sure these were not random events; I was convinced of that as I continued the work, and could see the connections and interlocking stories among all of the narratives.

Many experiencers had been abused. Many expressed an interest, directly or indirectly, in exploring other realms. Many asked to be taken there—indeed almost appeared to be in training for the experience earlier in their lives.

Intent seems to play a major role here. But let's examine some of the cases closely.

The Universe Hears an Appeal: Evelyn Carleton

If you recall from the Preface, mere hours before she received her NDE, Evelyn Carleton looked to the sky and demanded, "God, if there is something more, show it to me. I won't take one more step forward until you show me some answers." Could we say that Evelyn asked for her NDE?

I've discovered that many NDErs ask directly—even demand—that they be shown something to prove there is more to life than what they are experiencing on earth. Many reach into the depths of their soul to send a direct message to the universe, and in some cases, the universe complies. All of the NDErs in this study asked—in their way—for the experience. The experiences weren't accidents, and in fact, seemed very intentional. The signs suggest their NDEs were manifested.

Evelyn asked directly for a shift to her reality. Is it possible that under the right circumstances the universe can step in, select someone to fulfill a higher purpose, create an NDE, and send that person back to do the universe's work? Evelyn said she had always felt different, as if she didn't fit in. That feeling led her to look for an alternative to her current circumstances. She asked to be taken out of her reality, to find something better.

Did Evelyn elect herself as a candidate for an NDE? A vessel to be filled up for a higher purpose? Did she have an unconscious sense that she could be transformed and desired a type of transformational experience? Had she asked for another way of existence that would be more satisfying, more meaningful, more in tune for a person who felt ill-suited to life on our earth plane? In Evelyn's case, the time period between when she requested this and her NDE was just a few hours. Coincidence?

Or was this the universe's answer, to let her know there was more out there and that the universe would take over from there? That they would fill her with universal properties and return her to this plane? Was this their response?

An Indirect Case of Intention: Bob Magrisso

Another experiencer, Bob Magrisso (see Chapter 6), began to go down his path of spirituality years before his NDE. We can look to him to help reveal answers.

Like others, Bob had been moving in the direction of his NDE for years and his result seemed very intentional. In other words, he wanted a change and he got it.

When I asked Bob how his experience changed his life, he said, "It deepened it." His NDE altered the way he lives on a day-to-day basis and made him constantly examine his links with the Other. His life is spiritually based, from his medical practice to his path beyond his work. His life is entwined with the universe, 24/7.

At the time Bob had his NDE, he was seeing a Jungian analyst and was already involved in exploring the unconscious elements of his psyche. Bob was already a seeker, on a journey to work with his mind in a different way and explore the application of spiritual ideals to his daily life. He was in pursuit of a greater awareness, examining spirituality through various individual and group practices. Did Bob's work "grease the wheels" for the universe?

When I read for Bob, I was shown a pattern that became familiar as I spoke with other NDErs. Like others, Bob was stuck. At the time, I wondered if his pattern would be common in other experiencers, and if so, what did it mean? I had been trained to pay attention to patterns, to changes, and to trends, so this was practically begging for me to examine it.

From what I've gathered, I can say there seems to be an inflection point when NDEs occur. Many experiencers have had emotional trauma, but they also have the capability for a more satisfying existence. But they don't know how to get there, or they can't get there, at least on their own. At a certain point—a turning point—they are pulled out of their bodies to be re-awakened. The universe appears to play a role and the result is not completely within the bounds of the individual. They later return to life on earth to carry on, but, on an alternative path and a higher purpose. It's fair to say that many of them don't know they have a higher purpose and, if they sense it, might not be able to identify it. This turning point and its aftermath can be traumatic in itself and not lead to a peaceful existence. We'll examine this condition and mission more closely shortly.

For Bob, his interest in spirituality was reinforced following his NDE, as his art practice blossomed to convey a message. "This experience validated so much and gave a reality to some of the things I'd meditated about," Bob said. It was an affirmation for him. And an affirmation for me, as well.

But did Bob manifest his experience? Was he an accomplice, co-creating his NDE? And what about others? Did others produce their experiences, too?

Profile of a Candidate in Readiness: Lewis Brown Griggs

Lewis Brown Griggs (see Chapter 4) was foundering before his NDE and his life wasn't getting any better. It seemed he'd reached an inflection point and outside circumstances interceded. Or, could we look at this another way and ask if Lewis played a more active role?

It seemed as if many of these individuals are on a kind of radar screen for vulnerable people, those who are susceptible, but also could give so much more if given the chance. In a sense, these are individuals who are ready and could be turned for a larger purpose—a life of more sweeping meaning and contribution.

When I examined what I'd learned about NDEs and about Lewis, it seemed he did have certain qualities that culled him out as a candidate.

For example, on the outside, Lewis was a success. Internally, he could never quite come into his power, held back by his birthright and upbringing. While Lewis seemed to have the greatest assets in the world, his life was stuck in neutral as he tried to break out of the confines of his background.

And then Lewis had his NDE. And was sent back to do a mission like others. Which Lewis did. He found his niche.

Did Lewis manifest his NDE? Though he did not ask directly, his life appeared to be lined up for an unintentional event. He was in a groove he couldn't quite pull out of. The conventional means to deal with his life—money, prestige, class—weren't quite working for him. He needed something more—something more powerful.

Something else was delivered. Something farther afield than the conventional trappings he was accustomed to and that many of us use to define our lives. Things like money, power, status, and prestige. These are earthly solutions but not solutions for the universe.

Explorer on the Edge: Dan Rhema

Before his NDE, Dan Rhema (see Chapter 6) was always looking for the next new thing, beyond the mainstream. The farther away the better. Was Dan a candidate for his NDE *because* he was an explorer? Because his NDE was the ultimate exploration—one he would never find on earth.

We can also ask if Dan was set up for his journey. Was it pre-arranged, set in motion through universal intervention? Was his NDE waiting in the wings, for that precise moment when his physical trauma and his life's journey converged at an exquisitely perfect moment only the universe could pinpoint?

We can also ask if Dan's NDE happened at a sweet spot in his life, a time when he felt compelled to return due to family responsibilities. When Dan was given a choice to stay or return, he evaluated it and decided to come back, specifically for his wife and children. Like Ana Callan (see Chapter 15), Dan was far enough along in his life path and maturity to weigh the consequences of not coming back and decided to be of service to the universe. Not only did Dan appear to be on a path as a candidate, but timing also appears to be a factor here.

"I want to know more about these things that no one understands—these mysteries we don't have answers for," Dan says. Dan kept searching, but was thwarted until he was given the answer that he was looking for and that changed his life.

We still don't know the answers to the many questions that come up about NDEs, but the cases in books such as *Life After Near Death*, like Dan's, lead us to ask if he, and others, were priming themselves for a paradigm shift? Was Dan feeling around in the dark, waiting to be accessed, that is, delivered up for a mission as he moved away from convention in search of an alternative?

What Type of Person Is a Candidate for an NDE?

Most of the experiencers fell into the group of folks who grew up thinking, *I'm different.* As adults they still feel the same way: *I don't feel like I belong. I don't fit in.* They live with this awareness, but always, in the back of their mind, or even more present, are the thoughts/questions: *Is there something else? Can I experience another reality?* Through the cases in this book, we discover that many of these individuals push that thought to the extreme, in order to explore other possibilities and other realities. They take themselves out of their bodies, attempt to leave in some way, and at some point find themselves beyond this reality, delivered there through some other force.

It is also apparent that NDErs must be a certain type of individual. A pattern of childhood abuse appears to be a prerequisite, perhaps because it contributes to that trait of vulnerability that they share. They also must be willing to pursue a mission with all their heart and soul. Of course these individuals must also be capable of grasping the profound changes they undergo and rebalance themselves to a new, spiritually oriented service.

It's also occurred to me that for those who suffered childhood abuse, this could be the universe's way of saying, "We've got your back. We'll take over from here."

"Give me something that's out there. I'm up for it," many NDErs seem to say. "This can't be all there is."

On the other hand, these men and women may not necessarily be expecting the torpedo that completely re-orders their lives. And not all of them can handle it.

A Cycle of Abuse: Barbara Whitfield

In my reading with Barbara Whitfield (see Chapter 3), I asked about her childhood and she said, "Yes, you're right. I suffered from abuse. I had forgotten that I used to go into the tunnel as a child after I had been abused."

"You kept creeping in there before your NDE?" I asked, realizing I was hearing something significant.

"Right," she said.

This meant that Barbara had already opened the door to a different reality—and as a youngster crept through it. So, when her NDE finally occurred, she was already experimenting with entering a portal to a separate world.

"I had forgotten that," Barbara said.

Barbara developed a process of leaving this world behind through a ritual. Did that serve as a way to prime the pump for an eventual break in a more complete way during her NDE?

Exploring Alternate Realities: Ken Ebert

Ken Ebert (see Chapter 10) is another NDEr who was involved in exploring his consciousness for years prior to his NDE. He knew there was something else out there and wanted to find out what it was. Long before the accident that led to the NDE, Ken had already opened the door and was reading books and exploring other places in his mind. Ken liked to think about what was on the other side of that consciousness door and wanted to go there. Still, when it finally showed up, he wanted proof that other realities existed. He wanted to make sure he wasn't just using his imagination and making it all up.

Similar to other candidates, individuals like Ken are already creeping or directly advancing toward another realm. Those who express a desire, to either leave our world, to know more, or to delve into a more satisfying existence, one for which they are better suited, appear to be making themselves candidates. At the same time, these individuals sense they are not fulfilling their purpose on earth, leading to a sense of frustration and contributing to a sense of not belonging.

Within the NDErs I worked with, there exists a certain combination of raw material that can be put to better use; that with the desire to have an experience out in the universe tend to be qualities that blend to create the profile of an NDE candidate.

Ken admitted he was aimless before his NDE, despite being talented and possessing tremendous ability. He was aware of not using any of it, at least not in the way he should have.

Ken confirmed this but also acknowledged that, at the same time, he'd been exploring other worlds. His consciousness was open and he was exploring it—not to the extent he would later in life. The door was open and he'd begun reading materials that he hoped would take him to that other realm. Still the universe couldn't quite get his attention.

Ken agreed, telling me that the very first book he read on his own was *A Wrinkle In Time*, a story about a troublesome student who is capable of great things and is transported to another universe that weaves together time and space. The author, Madelyn L'Engle, wrote the book in the late 1950s, during a time of her own personal transition, when she herself was studying quantum physics.

In Ken's reading I was told, *You were already exploring these other places in your mind and you knew there was a possibility for something else. You liked to think about that and go there. And you imagined it and considered it a lot. At the same time, you were a very capable guy and weren't using all of your talents. You were doing some not very intelligent things.*

"Yes, a few," Ken agreed.

Things that weren't going anywhere, that didn't add to you.

"Yes," he repeated.

Ken realized his life wasn't building on any of his strong qualities, which would have allowed him to be of greater use to the universe.

Ken kept entertaining the idea that there was something else "out there" and got close to it, through reading and imagining. He didn't exactly wish for it, but he *kind of* wished that a part of him could be there.

"I wished I could be there and when it finally showed up," Ken said, "and I was nose to nose with it, I challenged it. Any time I ran up against it, I said 'I see you. Now *show me.*'"

Whether they're creeping toward this other realm, or rapidly advancing, NDErs are individuals who express a desire to leave the limits of our reality or have a greater experience in the universe. They are selected through their voluntary or involuntary qualities, and then recruited by the universe to do its work. These candidates were skimming rock bottom and living unsatisfying lives. And when they had the opportunity, it was up to them to convert their journey for the universe. But are the facts always as clear as in Ken's case?

A Breach to Transformation: Mary Ann Mernaugh

I discovered that same rocky pattern in childhood for Mary Ann Mernaugh (see Chapter 14), who had difficulties growing up and as a young woman. The timing of Mary Ann's NDE appeared to be related to the rest of her life, almost as if she was going along and, at a key moment, she was jabbed and shown a more evolved alternative. A force was trying to get her attention and say, "Look! Here's a different way."

On the outside, Mary Ann was struggling to be the wholesome girl from the Midwest. The All-American image was a bit of an effort, though, because underneath, Mary Ann had lots of questions.

Mary Ann had a stressful marriage and a father who had passed away, and she'd had a child who died. All of these traumas can lead to a crack in our protective armor, the fabric of our emotional structure. Is this the crack the universe is waiting for to enter to do its work? Because it appears as if that entry point is key.

Mary Ann admits she was the rare teenager who didn't care what her peers thought; she confronted bullies and followed her own path. Was this the type of raw material that could be used for a higher purpose? Perhaps the universe evaluated Mary Ann and said, "Here is someone who could be of service."

A Famous Tale of Manifestation From Popular Culture

In popular culture, there are many well-known examples of NDEs. It's a significant theme across the arts.

According to Alan Pew, writing in The Significance of the Near-Death Experience in Western Cultural Traditions, the 1951 short story "A Descent into the Maelstrom," by Edgar Allan Poe, contains a number of elements of the NDE, including a spellbinding description of the border of an idyllic world, ineffability, a reluctance to tell others, and a major transformation in the protagonist's values and attitudes toward life.[1] In another example, Ambrose Bierce describes the NDE in "An Occurrence at Owl Creek Bridge," a story written in 1891, 84 years before Moody's description of the NDE, which includes the tunnel, a loud buzzing at the moment of death, meetings with spirits of loved ones, and a border.[2]

In addition, within Jonathan Swift's *Gulliver's Travels*, Lewis Carroll's twin tales *Alice in Wonderland* and *Through the Looking Glass*, J.M. Barrie's *Peter Pan*, and C.S. Lewis's *The Lion, the Witch and the Wardrobe*, the protagonists are shown to travel to fantastic other worlds inhabited by a variety of strange and interesting beings.

Let's also take a look at Frank Baum's *The Wizard of Oz*, a book (and film) that's all about a journey, exploration, and conversion, and that has a special message that I particularly like about manifestation and intent.

The Wizard of Oz is complete with a surreal landscape, Dorothy's amazing friends (who resemble her real-life friends and relatives), and gifts such as the ruby slippers. But the film is also an exploration of intent and manifestation.

Dorothy expresses her desire to leave her "home." She is looking for an improvement in her ordinary reality, which we have to admit, in Kansas, looks pretty boring.

Dorothy's "wish" is granted and she is transported to another realm, where she is shown properties that don't exist on earth. Unusual landscapes and beings with supernatural powers that exist "over the rainbow." She is told to follow her path (the "yellow brick road") and ultimately discovers that the answers she is seeking lie within her—that the capacity for her journey existed all along. After her adventures, Dorothy is given a gift—the ruby slippers—and returns "home," transformed. She is no longer dissatisfied. She tries to tell her relatives about her strange journey, but they just laugh, much like the reaction to modern-day NDErs. Yet Dorothy knows that what she experienced was real and she carries it and her transformation with her forever.

Whether we ourselves have one or not, there's a universal meaning for NDEs that's been examined throughout the ages.

Manifestation Through the Lens of Science

NDEs ultimately lead back to age-old questions: Are consciousness and the physical world somehow connected? Do we co-create our realities through our minds? Does collective consciousness exist and do we each contribute to our unified existence? Do we exist in a world that can be created?

We have seen that many NDErs claim dissatisfaction with the familiar and the ordinary, which leads them to seek alternatives in the unexplored, the under-investigated. They ask for it—in some cases, plead for it. And it works. Their appeals are answered.

When we ask or demand what we want, we often receive the most direct and rapid results. We can ask as a prayer or with more focused intent, but when many go to the brink and ask for help, that's when they get results. This is called manifestation.

According to Imants Barušs, PhD, at King's University College, a "layer of deep consciousness gives rise to intentional consciousness and physical manifestation," as reported in the *Journal of Cosmology* in 2009.[3] According to author and scientist Dean Radin, "Over the course of the past 75 years, there has been a gradual accumulation of empirical evidence in support of a direct connection between mentally expressed intention and physical manifestation."[4] This suggests that consciousness is an additional element to matter—or that matter itself is a byproduct of consciousness.[5,6]

It is not known if this extends to the manifestation of an NDE, but evidentiary evidence points us in that direction.

According to Baruss, writing in the Journal of Cosmology in 2009, "The conventional research programs for understanding consciousness as an emergent property have failed to deliver."[7] For example, as one of the developers of functionalist cognitive theories has said, "The last forty or fifty years have demonstrated that there are aspects of higher mental processes into which the current computational models, theories, and experimental techniques offers vanishingly little insight."[8]

Are we magnets—energetic conductors—able to attract that which we desire? Is a possible way to look at manifestation through the lens of the magnetic field? Einstein considered the fields of magnetism and electricity in his physics in 1905, the time frame in which he explored the concept of a magnet at rest and the electrical field surrounding it. So, can we extrapolate and ask if we, too, are energetic, a type of magnet and manifestation is the effect of the magnetic energy we create in our fields?

For some time, physicists have been exploring the relationship between human consciousness and its relationship to the structure of matter. According to Rupert Sheldrake, "The answer might lie in the notion of morphic fields, patterns that are not themselves physical, but that physical manifestation follows."[9] Some empirical evidence exists to support the existence of such fields, which can be created by volition acting at the level of deep consciousness. Sheldrake's morphogenesis theory implies that intention is not a unique trait of human consciousness, but an essential part of all life in biological systems.

This book points to the same conclusion: Intention, at the level of deep consciousness, persists across the universe. The power of the mind is remarkable and, with the right direction, can create expressions in behavior. There is sufficient evidence to take seriously the notion that direct effects of intention on manifestation exist.

The cases in this book include men and women who have lived their lives with patterns of behavior that have existed for many years. The results, the NDEs, didn't occur after a few episodes of these folks wishing for something better. So a word of warning: Don't try this at home and expect immediate results. It won't work. And remember: The universe appears to contribute an element to this experience as well.

Manifestation Today

Today, manifestation is taught by imagining what life would look like when an intention is realized. Sometimes, winks from the universe occur after an intention is set. These winks may take the form of messages, synchronicities, new opportunities, or answers that begin to emerge. Whether we recognize them or not, most of us are on the receiving end of these phenomena; they aren't reserved just for "special" individuals.

According to Swiss psychiatrist Carl Jung in *Synchronicity: An Acausal Connecting Principle*, synchronicities are signs of something powerful moving deeply in the unconscious mind when two worlds, the inner and outer, are aligned.[10] Are these synchronicities just random events in our lives no more consequential than a random conversation in passing with a colleague? Or, are these occurrences the result of deep and profound connections between consciousness and the world of matter?

It appears that something very powerful seems to be happening behind the scenes. Strands of consciousness form and weave together to converge into a whole that delivers up our intent from the realm of space and time, from which the universe is comprised.

Quantum physics is just beginning to propose that the human mind has the power to manifest or co-create the outcomes of our own realities. The evidentiary evidence of the NDE seems to confirm this and suggests that the flow of energy plays a part. So, is it possible the NDErs create a strong, concentrated, energy that can transport them to another realm through a significant enough production of intent?

According to Harvard psychologist Ellen Langer, most people seek facts and regard their knowledge as absolute.[11] In fact, the more "black and white," we are in our thinking, the more logical view of the universe we hold. The more smug and righteous we are in our beliefs, the less likely these messages seem to occur. Staying with the familiar seems to keep us fixed because of what our minds do with it. NDErs appear to pursue alternate scenarios as a natural occurrence, as seekers of the alternate by nature, driven to find other ways of being.

Is this your path, too? Are you a candidate for manifestation? As you have probably seen in your life already, you must really mean it when you ask for your heart's desire. You must be emotionally vested when you set your intent. But be careful what you chose to create. You might create a journey to another reality.

17 * The Meaning of Consciousness in the NDE Experience *

"Deep down the consciousness of man
is one."
—David Boehm

As I moved forward with this work, I realized I was tapping into only the thinnest crack in the veneer of consciousness. A fragile opening, yet I knew there was more.

This work also led me to greater questions. Is the untold vastness of stars, planets, and galaxies that extends across millions of light years somehow linked to the creation of consciousness? Is consciousness at an unimaginable scale, yet no scale at all? How does what we know about consciousness impact our understanding of death, the afterlife, eternity, and oneness?

There were many striking moments in this research. One of the most memorable was our assumptions regarding how we connect with reality. All of us on earth make this basic assumption, and most of us think of reality as what we touch and feel and see—what we receive through our physical senses. Yet, the real mystery lies outside of this reality. Our consciousness is lodged in our dense, physical bodies, which means we are never fully conscious until our consciousness separates at death. Or in an NDE or other transformative experience, when it is freed up to be completely available.

Consciousness is the most complex event of our existence, the last frontier that has not been sufficiently explored. Today, after extensive scientific study, nobody has the slightest idea how anything material could be conscious. The origin of the universe and consciousness is still one huge mystery to us.

Science and Consciousness

Consciousness is paradoxical. It is intangible, yet we know it exists. We have no idea how it is put together, because we can't see it, but we know it is front and center in our lives, our frame of reference for how we regulate our lives.

What about the brain, the instrument panel for the scientific view of consciousness? How does the brain explain our subjective experience? According to conventional thinking, when scientists talk about consciousness, they refer to the brain. According to science, Rajiv Parti's veridical experience (viewing his sister and his mother in India drinking tea while he was halfway around the world on an operating table at UCLA Medical Center; see Chapter 5) could not have occurred. But it did. Looked at through the lens of science, when Barbara Whitfield was lying in her hospital bed (see Chapter 3), she could not have overheard a conversation at the nursing station down the hall. But she did.

Current scientific thinking is built on the premise that we can't trust evidence you can't test. But the energetic world eludes scientific research and checking. It is intangible. It does not play by the same rules as the conventional, material world even though science persists in applying our physical laws to it.

Is it possible that the answer to consciousness does not lie in the brain? That all existence is lodged elsewhere? That the characteristic that gives us life and knowing, that element of the NDE that is ineffable, may reside elsewhere? Within us? Or around us? That it is eternal and integrated within the universe?

Examining consciousness began as far back as 350 BCE when Aristotle and Plato agreed on the principle that multiple souls encompassed several functions, including one that controls biological functions, another that controls feelings, and yet another that controls the ability to reason. By the 1600s, Rene Descartes began to contemplate the issue. There had to be not just a physical realm but a mental realm, he reasoned. He believed in dualism—that mind and body are not equivalent.

In our contemporary world, science focuses on consciousness as a consequence of our physicality. Brain death explains the end of life as we know it, scientists say. NDEs are nothing but a series of brain reactions. But scientific explanations are lacking in the realm of the NDE. The story the scientific world tells simply does not hang together. It not only does not explain consciousness, it does not begin to explain the near-death experience.

As you have seen in this book, consciousness as encountered by the NDErs is a realm not defined by materialism, not made of matter, at least not matter by our definition. It's a realm that eludes explanation and our current tools of measurement.

According to the cases in this book, universal consciousness is pulling all sorts of strings at every moment in our existence unknown to us. NDEs are just a small part of what's happening in consciousness. Our universe is a little pocket in a much vaster space, a space we cannot fathom, a larger, more complex whole.

We are tapped into a collective form of knowing that we cannot contemplate.

As we examine reality, we must ask: Can the mystery of reality be attributed to the moment when pure consciousness meets universal consciousness? Is our consciousness more acute, and more real and substantial when not filtered or weighed down by our physical body? When this moment occurs, is this the exquisite moment of all knowing—the total comprehension we are seeking? And are we therefore immortal and infinite in time and space?

The concept of reality and the search for our ultimate reality has dogged human beings since we noticed the celestial heavens above us. Much of our human existence is devoted to trying to make sense of our place in the universe and the role and interaction we have *within* that reality. Various schools of philosophical, spiritual, and scientific thought have attempted to explain this dominant question of human existence, this boundless mist of energy interwoven with the universe.

An Explanation of Consciousness Through the NDE

According to this work, consciousness is alive and surrounds us. Everything has some level of consciousness, and consciousness exists in all life. By virtue of rubbing up against it, we are imparted with consciousness.

It doesn't necessarily get into our physical body and doesn't reside in a physical location, and that's where science has a dilemma.

Consciousness is invisible. It's permeable, like the air, and doesn't have to reside in a physical place: the brain, the heart, or a physical organ. It seeps through us like steam so it doesn't have to be in the brain. It doesn't have to be in the heart. It doesn't have to be anywhere. Because it's porous, it's thin. It's not of our concrete world. The emerging evidence shows that our consciousness is without borders and our views of the afterlife must be re-examined.

In universal consciousness, everything is recorded in a system based on non-physicality and non-locality. We can't impose our laws on that system. Our world, our reality, is a snapshot, a series of vignettes, created by consciousness. It's like a file or Rolodex that is a subset of the totality of the universe. Everything in consciousness can be drawn up, recreated and retrieved, but never lost.

In this plane of "existence," there is stored information, a recording of every act, every behavior, that exists. This information is connected by the fiber, the invisible web that acts like a mesh to weave and record all beings together in an overwhelming, coordinated scheme.

In this way, all of our planets, our universe, everything that is in the universe is consciousness and consciousness is in everything.

What Happens When NDErs Return With an Extraordinary Boost of Consciousness?

NDErs' energy and consciousness are altered permanently when they return—an impact that cannot be overstated. This alteration affects their powers, their behavior, and their day-to-day existence. Prior to their NDEs, these individuals existed in the state of equilibrium we associate with life on earth—their proportion of physicality/consciousness was stable. However, following their NDEs, they return top-heavy. Their increased consciousness is an unwieldy assignment, an unfamiliar way of being for most. There is no way to execute, often no game plan or strategy, for this new blend. They're on their own.

For NDErs, it's as if they left the room, and when they returned, they were in a different room, in a different house, in a different world. They were gone for only an instant, but when they returned, they weren't the same and everything had changed. The NDErs' minds expanded when they left their physical bodies behind, until their consciousness merged with the universe and they were one and the same.

"You're not really in control of the state," Bob Magrisso says (see Chapter 6). "It's somewhat like you're taken there and you have a strong sense of leaving the normal plane of existence. It's the sense that you're part of something bigger."

To provide some context, keep in mind that Western science says that the experiences that NDErs relate are not real. Science's first inclination is to cut these experiences down to size. *This really didn't happen* is the judgment served up with a side of skepticism. In many cases, we see outright denial that these events occurred. Or maybe they're drug-induced hallucinations or malfunctions of the brain. Yet, it's uncanny that all the delusions are identical among the experiencers. The scientific community is unable to definitively explain what's happening or understand how the brain could cause these after-effects.

Consciousness is not human or alive. It is made up of infinity and no time; all space and no space. It arose from the force of a multitude of modalities, the planets, and some universal alchemy far off in a universe, billions of years ago, Spirit seemed to whisper. It was not created in any lifetimes we can understand.

It's a power that has intent over everything: a specific realm that engages all the senses—yet at the same time, you have no senses when you are there. You're able to respond and take in everything it has to offer, and what it has to offer is everything—every element: music, spirituality, the ability to see our loved ones, a castle beyond comprehension. It's like dipping into earthly properties of an immense proportion.

Consciousness is our essence. The physical bodies we wear on earth are temporary vehicles for us to experience life on a three-dimensional plane. Once we leave this earth, we exist as pure consciousness, pure essence. We can connect to everything by virtue of the fact that we are not restricted by physicality.

The question of consciousness, the ineffable alteration of our reality, is a unique one. Examining it through the lens of an NDE increases its complexity. Experiencers spoke of the puzzle of reality and how the reality of the NDE was more real than the reality of our earth. This leads to the question: Is our reality nothing more than a token to satisfy our limited understanding of our existence?

More Real Than Reality Itself

Once we move beyond the physical density of our bodies, can we clearly experience true universal reality? This question has been explored by scientists over time, and philosophy and literature have a lot to say about this intersection:

* ✳ "Reality is merely an illusion albeit a very persistent one." (Albert Einstein)

* ✳ "Everything we call real is made of things that cannot be regarded as real." (Niels Bohr)

* ✳ "There are things known and there are things unknown, and in between are the doors of perception." (Aldous Huxley)

* ✳ "If the doors of perception were cleansed everything would appear to man as it is, infinite." (William Blake)

* ✳ "Humankind cannot bear very much reality." (T.S. Eliot)

* ✳ "Nothing exists except atoms and empty space; everything else is opinion." (Democritus)

* ✳ "The human understanding is like a false mirror, which, receiving rays irregularly, distorts and discolors the nature of things by mingling its own nature with it." (Francis Bacon)

Each NDEr shared similar experiences in their interactions with the universe and consciousness. As Dan Rhema said, "I would have really intense dreams. It's hard to explain to people what my nights can be like. I got there [the experience] in just a moment in time but after that it took me a long time to try to process what happened because it was against everything I used to think. I had to really work my way into this saying, 'That's okay. It's all right for me to do this kind of thing.'"

"The NDE is a living thing and it doesn't just stop after you have it and that's the end of it," I told Dan. "The process goes on for the rest of your life."

And although it sounds great to some, the experience of eternal consciousness is not all it's cracked up to be. For NDErs, there is no relief—no time when they are not assaulted by unwanted consciousness. Yet, they also say our reality seems flat by comparison. As I discussed this issue with them, I learned more about their gradual acceptance of this event. Some were further along in the process than others. Many didn't understand what was happening initially. Some asked for information from me and, in my role, I was able to tell them what I had learned from other experiencers. I could tell them that all the NDErs I'd met learned to adjust—some more completely than others—and that it required time.

In my conversations with NDErs, I told them that when you enter that other reality following your NDE, your experiences can be unusual. When some of these men and women go to sleep or close their eyes, they might see faces or hear music. They're connecting on a different level. A few NDErs told me that they awaken at night and are careful not to wake their spouses as they go to another room to allow this process to unfold. They watch and listen as observers to an unseen world.

Consciousness as Mission

What is "mission" and why is it prevalent in the NDE experience?

Mission comes from the Latin word *mittere*, which means "to send." And this concept of being sent to do work, couldn't be more true for the NDErs who appear to return after their experience to become delegates on behalf of the universe.

Missions appear throughout history and are found in the folklore of many cultures. Executing a mission requires great fortitude, great exertion, and the overcoming of many obstacles; the same is true for the NDErs who find that their true work hasn't begun until they return.

Mission appears to be the universe's attempt to implant a specific intent in the NDEr's consciousness. When NDErs return, they not only return with a variety of after-effects, they return with a new direction. This goes beyond a sortie or the desire to find the meaning in life that so many of us yearn for. This is the universe's consciousness, deep seated and a compulsivity that is embedded within them. They return as the light, with switched on abilities that we are usually ascribe to higher powers. They pile up one against another, to bring about a change in how the planet operates.

How Is Mission Created?

At some point after the near-death experience, the person returns to life. As you've no doubt noted, they may have been given a choice or may find themselves jolted back into their bodies. They may say they returned because their life's work was not complete. Or their return may have stemmed from a sense of responsibility, such as not wanting to leave their family, as it was for Dan Rhema (see Chapter 6).

The experiencer may be given a reason why he must return, such as "It's not your time." Some are told of a specific mission, like Lewis Brown Griggs (see Chapter 4). Others have the sense that they were given a mission, but for the life of them, can't remember what it is, like Mary Ann Mernaugh (see Chapter 14). Some know they have work to do, feel a compulsion to do it and set off to become a beacon of light. It may be a concrete mission, as it is for Robert Bare, who states, "I only want to do good" (see Chapter 10), or it may be a mission to bring the resonance of the harp to the dying, "something bigger than me, bigger than the harp," like Marissa (see Chapter 12). Some missions are visible and others are uncertain.

Following the NDE, NDErs' lives change in ways they are not prepared for. They have to think, act, and live differently. They must put it all together in the correct way and put that new system into effect to help us all. The outcome, if it works well, becomes their mission. The underlying theme to serve humanity is a constant. So is the compulsiveness with which they discharge their work. For some it's less of a leap than a progression but still, it is an exploration downloaded and guided by Spirit.

What is the universe telling us about our earth? Why are "they" sending back batteries of consciousness to light our planet? What does the universe know about our earth and its future? And will we on earth understand the message? These questions remain, even as we explore the answers.

18 * *Everything Is Energy* *

> "To understand the true nature
> of the universe, one must think
> in terms of energy, frequency
> and vibration."
> —Nikola Tesla

As you've seen, my work in *Life After Near Death* led me in many different directions, introducing me to a variety of new clues along the way.

I began this work focused on solving the riddle of NDE after-effects. As I began the research, I attempted to delve into the essential nature of what happens in an NDE, its after-effects, and the meaning for all of us. I ended up going much further, investigating the mysteries of consciousness and the energetic realm, the nature of "the life to come" and the life force that exists in all of us.

The notion of energy infuses the realm of the NDE. Everything the experiencers return with is a result of entering a higher frequency energetic range, a non-material realm we can't define and have difficulty addressing in our spoken language. In the language of the NDE and the readings, this realm is indeed the "light." Yet it also encompasses the resulting after-effects.

At first, these after-effects seemed inexplicable, but with more probing, they took on a greater coherence. An enhanced, undeniable effect results from being in the "light." This effect selectively strengthens our abilities, boosts our healing, amplifies our intelligence, heals our physicality, intensifies our experiences, and upgrades our capacity. How do we explain this?

We Are Energy

One reason why NDEs are so powerful is that they expose and engage essential aspects of consciousness that are all but opaque in the day-to-day reality most of us experience. Accessing this space unveils more than anything we can imagine.

Our physical experience on earth is but one, very narrow aspect of the vastly larger reality that NDErs access. Every indication we have suggests that this "universal" reality emerges as a field of energy known by various names, including the One, Source, God, and Cosmic Consciousness, among others.

Although our human experience dramatically limits our ability to fully understand this greater reality, many sources explain that our consciousness derives from this field, and is directly connected to and interacts with it. It is one unimaginably large, integrated, amazingly complex concentration of energy. Our consciousness, being an integral aspect, never dies, and our essence exists in tandem for perpetuity and eternity.

When we pass, our consciousness exits the physical body we wear on earth, moving into this vast realm where this profound energetic activity occurs. We are able to experience higher knowledge, to partake in the All, to exist for all time—a concept clearly inconsistent with our present understanding of physical laws.

When we have an NDE, our essence leaves our physical body to experience a type of astrophysical event. Our consciousness returns to the physical reality of earth infused with the experience of this larger realm. All of the individuals in this study returned with altered awareness that reconfigured their physical existence with characteristics and abilities we call after-effects. We have no category of science to describe this phenomenon, but this could ultimately become the new physics—a study of an unknown energy and process, generated by a yet-unidentified source that alters our physical energy permanently.

The energy of the astral realm is unlike energy on earth—chemical, mechanical, nuclear, radiant, or electrical. These earthly energies are denser than the energy of the astral plane, which vibrates at an extremely high frequency. The density of the astral plane is virtually non-existent.

What Is Frequency?

Many sources, among them venerable philosophers and scholars, explicitly state that everything that exists, vibrates. This would mean that an essential nature of this vast realm is that it pulsates at different frequencies.

What is frequency? Frequency is the basic rate at which anything vibrates—the number of vibratory cycles per second (measured in Hertz, where 20 Hz would equal 20 cycles per second).

Our experience is that objects in our reality vary in frequency from (seemingly) zero to extremely high frequencies, like radio and light waves. Audio or sound waves vibrate at lower relative frequencies (thousands of times per second); radio waves are higher (millions per second); visible light is much higher; and x-rays and gamma rays vibrate faster still.

Because the differences in the field are essentially differences in vibratory patterns, by definition everything we experience is essentially the product of a combination of vibrations or frequencies.

Different types of materials (rocks, trees, and fire, for example) have different base frequencies upon which vibrations are superimposed to produce the extraordinary details we observe. The result is called a waveform, a combination of a great number of frequencies.

Like everything we observe, each part of our physical body has a signature waveform with its own frequency. The entire human body is a super complex waveform that includes the various frequencies and energetic signatures of its component parts. Very complex indeed.

These components can be isolated by base frequency. For instance, our cells vibrate at a base frequency of 1000 Hz. Our heart vibrates at a base frequency of 100 Hz. It's estimated that our overall physical body vibrates at a base frequency of 7–10 Hz.

Okay, you may be thinking to yourself now. *Where is she going with this? How does this relate to the NDE?*

As you can now imagine, our organs and the other major parts of our body are concentrations of vibratory activity—energetic centers—that, if influenced or changed, can influence the operation of the rest of the organism.

Light Waves and Energy

Some NDErs report experiencing colors of light that are impossible for them to describe in conventional terms, opening the distinct possibility that there are aspects of light or kinds of light of which we have no understanding. These lights and sources would almost certainly interact with whoever was exposed to them in ways that would be hard for us to understand.

There is also a common understanding that the spiritual realms are described by and operate at a significantly higher energetic frequency than those that produce our reality. The spiritual realm is generally described by an intensely bright "light." Yet at the same time, many admit that they understand or recognize this light as the One, the All, the universe, "God," and so forth. This "light" of Spirit appears to possess the highest frequency.

If we follow this train of thought, then, why wouldn't the white light of Spirit—a highly charged energetic phenomenon—have a significant impact on the NDErs that found themselves in that space? We can ask: Did this highly energetic light transform and alter them?

Patterns, Frequency, Vibration: The Connections

In Chapter 11, we discussed the Pattern that Lynnclaire Dennis received following her NDE. We also examined patterns in poetry, music, geometry, and math. In fact, pattern is integral to the concepts of waveforms that result from vibrations that comprise everything we see.

Throughout history, numerous clues and hints regarding energetic frequency have been staring at us, waiting for us to organize them like pieces of a giant puzzle. Here at the dawn of a new age, this puzzle is finally revealing the building blocks of a language based on energy, frequency, and form, which appear to be embedded in the NDE and its after-effects.

If there is such a thing as a universal language, can it be demonstrated in energetic patterns and vibrations? Patterns that already exist on earth—that are part of our lives? Does this language already exist? Can other information be conveyed through these patterns? Is frequency a way to create and tabulate the world around us? Clearly this concept has captivated thinkers and scientists for centuries. Nikola Tesla said, "If you want to find the secrets of the universe, think in terms of energy, frequency and vibration," and Einstein put it succinctly: "Everything is energy and that's all there is to it."

Vibrations are everywhere. We are surrounded by vibrations. We live in an ocean of vibrations. Vibrations move through us like sound travels through the ocean.

We are all woven together and to the universe by the invisible units of energy and vibration. We can think of them as millions of subatomic particles popping with energy. Everything seen and unseen in the Cosmos is stitched together through an energetic framework that exists according to its own laws. These experiences take place in a space so vast, so beyond our borders or tools, that we cannot yet define the specifics and don't have the vocabulary to put them in nicely slotted boxes.

The ability to be in the light, that higher vibration that all NDErs describe as the brilliant or bright white light, the "light of Spirit," can lead to amplification of earthly properties. The vibration generated by this frequency and energy can reach out and restore balance and raise our consciousness to altered states. This energy, this higher frequency that NDErs return with, can also express itself as gifts, heightened abilities, a high frequency transfusion that grants us talents.

Vibrational Energy

If you're like most of us, you're probably wondering, how you can raise your frequency without having an NDE? Every day methods include meditation, chanting, drumming, Tibetan singing bowls, and vocal toning. Hypnosis, a variation of trance, can also can be used to raise vibration. Some believe gratitude, expressions of love, and compassion can also raise vibrations. But be aware that you won't raise your frequency high enough to be in a near-death state. Indeed, you would not want to. You do not want to die or nearly die to achieve this state. Yes, it's possible to use these methods to raise your consciousness and to take another step forward, but not the final step forward.

The heightened frequency that NDErs achieve, such as picking up a faint radio signal that's out of listening range, is what has the ability to transform, mold, and forever alter them.

Science's Take on Energy and the Near-Death State

Scientists have examined energy and energetic manifestation but have largely seen it as incidental to the role of the brain in the near-death state. Yet, according to research at the University of Arizona, there is scientific evidence that electrical aspects of brain activity change through mystical and near-death experiences.[1]

Though scientists have focused on the brain in experiments of the afterlife, they have largely disregarded the key underlying element—the increased electrical activity registered at death and near-death states that runs throughout these experiences. Science focuses on the brain, but ignores the consistent fact that it is the electrical fields that are altered, whether in humans, in rats, or in other scientific studies.

According to research published in the *Proceedings of the National Academy of Sciences*, a study at the University of Michigan carried out on dying rats found high levels of brainwaves at the point of the animals' demise. The lead author of the study, "Electrical Signatures of Consciousness in the Dying Brain," concluded that in the 30-second period after the animals' hearts stopped beating, they measured a sharp increase in high-frequency brainwaves called gamma oscillations (the same gamma waves that bestowed Mary Ann Mernaugh with higher intelligence and were referred to in her case in Chapter 14).[2] In the rats, this unexplained surge in electrical connectivity was found at even higher levels just after the cardiac arrest than when animals were awake and well.

An electrical connection, the altered energy that occurs at death or near-death, is present. According to research in Zurich and meditation studies, high-frequency gamma waves are also connected to noetic experiences and meditation. It appears to be the electrical field itself that is the common denominator, that undergoes change at or near-death, and that leads to an alteration of energy. This theme calls for further study.

The Therapeutic, Transformative Effects of Energy and Frequency

When I began to piece together frequency, vibration, patterns, and energy, I realized NDE after-effects are connected to energy and energetic vibrations, and that the hidden language of the NDE is felt through the expression of rhythms, patterns, and vibrations as the experiencer travels through a landscape of lights and symbols.

NDEs are an energetic phenomena. Where the NDErs travel to, energy is infinite and immeasurable. A part of the NDEr steps out and is touched by that infinite energy. When NDErs return to earth, that energy is sewn into their being—a different frequency than what we're accustomed to on earth. The idea of the body as an energetic mechanism is not unique and is a unifying concept linking us to the universe. That higher frequency is carried in them like an implant, at the same time the physical body is still attuned to the earth's energy.

Energy ties together these NDE after-effects, which manifest as altered behavior and gifts. Music—sound and pattern on a frequency scale. Art—energy manifested as color and form. Vision—a function of light waves and frequency. Hearing—a function of sound waves and resonance. Math and geometry are both linked to energetic patterns. It appears that energetic waves or vibration are also involved in the healing qualities of an NDE. The higher frequency achieved by reorganizing matter at the base level revamps properties in the experiencer. NDE after-effects may appear to be talents but are, in fact, related to high frequency energetics.

What is it that's trying to be expressed through these patterns?

One answer is that somehow we have been guided toward a subconscious recognition of a grand pattern based on frequency, time, and space. Quite possibly, these expressions represent the building blocks of a language we do not fully understand but could be the language that underlies the structure of the universe.

Are NDEs the vehicle to convey us to a cosmic leap, a link between energetic vibration and the universe?

As I considered this question, I realized, I was arriving back full circle to where I began, to the time I had my first experiences with the psychic world and was told, "We're just energy and the energy has to go someplace."

19 ✳ *A New Paradigm to Explain the NDE* ✳

"The voyage of discovery is not in
seeking new landscapes but in having
new eyes."
—Marcel Proust

As I moved forward, I continued learning many new things. When I began this work, I expected to delve into the variety of near-death experience after-effects and satisfy my curiosity about their peculiar powers.

But something happened as the work unfolded: I realized the old paradigm to describe the event and its elements—the tunnel, the light, the beings—only comprised one level of the experience. I realized the elements could be built upon to examine the experience from a deeper level.

The elements have allowed scientists to classify the NDE. Yet, it's time to establish a deeper understanding of what else this phenomenon means beyond the spectacle of the elements. The knowledge that this experience is indeed real demands a greater understanding beyond the drama the experiencers recount.

With the best intentions, I went forward to catalogue near-death experience after-effects. But the universe had another plan in mind. It kept nudging me to look at other issues that it placed in front of me, in order to make me examine the deeper meaning of the NDE.

As I explored the cases, and delved into the world of consciousness beyond our grasp, I not only learned that the tangible powers the experiencers were left with didn't fit smoothly into my original plan but that all of these areas are intertwined. None stands alone. But as connected as they are, they can be overwhelming and best understood by taking each conclusion, separately.

15 Principles of the NDE

1. The NDE experience is an expression of energetic vibration.

2. Once the "door is blown open" for NDErs, consciousness and their connection with the universe are permanently accessible and unrestricted.

3. Post-NDE, connections to consciousness are involuntary. A disproportionate chunk of the experiencer's life is overwhelmed by consciousness.

4. NDErs are plugged into the universe after the experience, which means they are connected to all consciousness, causing heightened sensitivity.

5. NDEs appear to be manifested and brought about by intent.

6. The reality of the NDE is true consciousness and our reality on earth is only a slim reality.

7. NDErs appear to be in training and pre-selected by some unknown force for a larger mission.

8. The intent of an NDE appears to be to raise the consciousness of our planet.

9. Our consciousness lives forever, is universal, and controls all aspects of our lives. Our physical body is merely the temporary clothing we wear on earth.

10. The NDE alters energy for the experiencer upon their return.

11. The higher vibrational state of the NDE causes experiencers to interact and interfere with the electromagnetic plane upon return.

12. A life review in an NDE is given if there is an appropriate authority figure to deliver it, one the experiencer can respect, admire, and look up to.

13. The elements of the NDE are not the message of the NDE. The messages of the NDE are transformation and connection to universal consciousness.

14. Intentionally created altered states of consciousness do not guarantee an NDE.

15. Our consciousness exists outside our body after death in another state.

This information moves us beyond the initial first crack at the NDE 50 years ago. We are now ready to explore the next level.

20 ✳ *What Experiencers Have Learned, What I Have Learned,* ✳ *and What We Can All Learn Moving Forward*

"Maybe that's what life is...a wink of
the eye and winking stars."
—Jack Kerouac

All of the NDErs I worked with in my quest to understand the experience agree that life on earth is just one part of their astonishing journey and that what's on the "other side" vastly exceeds our most memorable earthly encounters. All the NDErs came back solid in their belief in the bigger picture and in the afterlife. They learned that we are all connected and all experiencing life on earth for a short time, and that the stresses we perceive to be insurmountable, when viewed from the perspective of the universe, are merely "earth problems."

The NDErs also learned that their old lives weren't options anymore. As this work progressed, I, too, realized I had come too far down this path to turn back. My old life was just that: my former life. I learned from those I encountered on the journey that these NDErs are inspirational in their ability to light the path for humankind. They helped me to keep going to write this book.

In this book, I have sought to unpack the meaning of near-death after-effects and the subsequent knotty branches that shoot out, which we regard as consciousness. Though I initially set out to explore the after-effects, it wasn't long before the path became entangled with the universe, a path that led me deeply into consciousness and its mysterious orbit.

Among the many things I learned was that inherent in the process of the NDE are patterns about consciousness and its meaning, which are repeated over and over. These conclusions, theories, and patterns are the pith of the book and take on a scientific, if not ethereal bent. I learned that this work has profound implications for our lives on earth and our understanding of reality. What I learned went far beyond my initial goal to take me into a realm of the grand order of things, the cosmos, the meaning of our lives after physical life, and the belief in other realities.

We are weighted down by our physical bodies and our senses while on earth. They prevent us from soaring to the heights of consciousness that can so easily create perfect bliss and perfection. Still, all of us have the ability and potential to enhance our lives. We don't need to wait to provoke a shift. The universe is calling for it now. We are all able to collaboratively soar; we have the ability and the tools to put it in place. Our contribution, at the individual level, is valuable. Even if we cannot reach the mystifying heights of the NDE, we can still move forward to have an impact on the universe.

We are all energetic beings connected to the universe and by the universe to each other. We can collectively launch ourselves into larger states of consciousness. Although we may not be able to reach the transformative levels of NDEs, we can use intentional enlightenment to connect to humanity and embark on a higher state of frequency to tune into a larger perspective. Each of us can shine a light on our planet.

What is it that's trying to be expressed through these patterns—the after-effects and powers of the NDE? We can logically ask if these patterns are the universe's way to call for a new consciousness.

The message of the NDE refers to the fact that we live/exist in an energetic/vibratory universe that underlies all of our activities, patterns, and actions. The NDE goes to the heart of our existence on earth and our relationship with the universe. The message is clearer in the NDE experience when we are unencumbered and not distracted by the physical sphere.

Prophets, mystics, and seers have predicted a time when man would make a cosmic leap into another realm of consciousness. Are NDEs the vehicles to convey us there?

My research has included devouring hundreds of books, articles, Websites, YouTube videos, movies, and interviews. I've been driven by curiosity about the questions that surround us and a passion to pursue this work. I kept moving forward even when others questioned what I was doing. If you have a dream, I realized, you've got to keep going. I tried to stay flexible and to see the opportunities that others might not.

I didn't have perfect answers to my larger questions at the outset of the journey, but as it progressed, I realized that perhaps no perfect answer exists, only pointers to new pathways and passages, new ways of examining the information.

As you can discern from my commentary in this book, my understanding of NDEs has shifted since I began this work and has taken on deeper meaning. The more digging I did and the more stories that others shared, the more the pieces fit together.

I continued to ask questions as the journey unfolded and to always find another way to pursue the questions—questions that run like threads in this book: *What knits the universe together? Does everything we see in an NDE account for everything that is? What is the nature of energy?*

Along the way, I became hooked. The work became a quest to explore our basic mysteries. And the journey allowed me to discover parts of myself in the process. As I came across patterns and stories that were nearly identical, I also learned that this is just the beginning of unpacking this experience and understanding the complexity of the NDE.

"We find our life by walking it," poet Maya Angelou said. Well, I walked my life. I never set out to do this. The journey became not only a tracking of the NDErs' personal journey, but my journey, too. Along the way I learned to accept my gifts, to use them to help others, and to say, "This is who I am."

The Universal Truths

I reiterate the universal truth that everything is truly energy. These stories and the unique after-effects convinced me that we are all part of something much bigger than any of us can contemplate or have the capability to express. And what we are a part of is complete and everlasting. These stories have introduced me to remarkable individuals who demonstrate that anything is possible and that our human capabilities are controlled in part by us, but more importantly by forces that we will never understand. We are all truly universal.

I've learned that I can't go back to looking at things the same way. Once you enter this realm, you discover that we don't live in a random or ho-hum material universe in which nothing much matters. In fact, we are laying the footprint for our universe through our actions and we collectively matter very much. I know that now.

Appendix A
The Terminology and Definition of a NDE

Raymond Moody, considered the "father" of the NDE, began to study near-death experiences when he was an 18-year-old philosophy major at the University of Virginia. While reading Plato's *The Republic*, he was intrigued by the story of Ur, a warrior thought dead who described going to another realm before returning to life.

"I felt the question of the afterlife was the black hole of the personal universe," Moody explained in his memoir, *Paranormal: My Life in Pursuit of the Afterlife*.[1]

Moody coined the term *near-death experience* to describe the after-death experience that many people claimed and recounted, but for which no research or proof existed. His book *Life After Life*, published in 1975, captured the public's interest and, since then, the public hasn't been able to get enough of this phenomenon.

According to Moody's definition, a near-death experience—or NDE—fits one of the following criteria:

* The experiences of a person who was resuscitated after having been thought, adjudged, or pronounced clinically dead by their doctors.

* The experiences of a person who, in the course of accidents or severe injury or illness, came very close to physical death.

* The experiences of a person who, as they died, told this to other people who were present. Later, these people reported the content of the death experience.

* A similar set of experiences—a tunnel of light, the sense that you're out of your body, a life review, a buzzing or ringing noise, a meeting with deceased loved ones, a profound sense of peace—before returning to the physical world.

Dr. Moody would soon be joined by other researchers in his quest to better understand near-death experiences.

Eight years after Dr. Moody published his book, Dr. Bruce Greyson elaborated on Moody's work. Greyson, a professor at the University of Virginia, developed a scale of 16 elements to measure the depth of an individual's near-death experience. According to Greyson's NDE-scale, a near-death-experience includes some of the following:

* Alteration in time.
* A sudden insight.
* A feeling of peace.
* A sense of unity with the universe.
* A brilliant light.
* Visions of the future.
* An out-of-body experience.
* Encountering a mystical being.
* Seeing deceased or religious spirits.
* Coming to a border, or point of no return.

According to Greyson, a score of at least seven on his Greyson scale qualifies the experiencer as a candidate for NDE research.

Sounds pretty definitive and conclusive. Right? But what if the explanation for a NDE lies outside our tools to measure? Could there be another way of looking at this?

In my experience, measuring the weightiness of someone's experience through the elements is not that simple. After all, this experience takes place in a realm that can't be measured or even detected by science. So can statistics be assigned to an experience in a non-material plane? Can consciousness be weighed and systematized? Put another way, can profundity be measured?

It is true that the elements provide a context to understand this intangible event, just as we search for language to describe the phenomenon, even if we don't have vocabulary adequate for the rest of the experience. The elements serve the purpose of providing a visual lexicon to access an experience that has been described by most as ineffable.

Yet, as I thought about the elements, I realized, to paraphrase Montoya, "I do not think it means what they think it means." The elements seemed to be only a sliver of the full meaning of the NDE. The message of the NDE seemed to encompass more, that we live/exist in an energetic universe that underlies all of our activities, patterns, and actions.

As work on NDEs has progressed, it's been discovered that the first medical report of a near-death experience is thought to have occurred in an 18th-century medical book written by a French military physician. *Anecdotes de Médecine* reportedly describes the case of a well-known pharmacist in Paris who, temporarily fell unconscious and reported seeing a "light so pure and bright he thought he must have been in Heaven."[2] This explanation is surprising because, at the time, most people relied on religion to explain the near-death experience.

NDEs also illuminate the concept that death and dying is not one cut-and-dried phenomenon. Whereas it's true that in our culture, death is considered the end of the physical body, the end of life, the question of the afterlife lingers. Can life continue? Perhaps not as we know it, but in a vaster realm?

It may be useful to think of this unseen realm as a prism. You can turn it every way but never fully see inside of it. Each way you turn it, you see another facet, another feature, all connected, yet all mysterious.

Methodology and First Steps

As time went on, the questions that motivated me to pursue this work continued: *What are near-death experience after-effects? How do experiencers acquire them? What are there implications? Why do so many people experience a return to life with traits completely foreign to them?* As you have seen from the text, these questions led me to dig in deeper.

Before I interviewed the experiencers, though, I thought about the type of methodology I would use in this research. I decided to model it on the type of research I was familiar with, and, in that way, make use of my talents and gifts. I chose qualitative research in which information is captured in various ways in order to record the experience and absorb as much as possible from the situation.

I had already begun research into the field to uncover the existing body of knowledge, reading Raymond Moody's books and others, and reviewing published cases. I would use rigorous qualitative methodology based on in-depth interviews, questionnaires, and case studies. I'd find the experiencers—the term used in the near-death field—and then investigate the cases and examine correlations and relationships among experiencers. When the interviews and questionnaires were complete, I would perform a reading to uncover information not readily accessible through the interviews and questionnaires. Finally, I would synthesize all the information to examine correlations and relationships among experiencers.

I would end up working with a universe of about 50 individuals who had experienced NDE's. I selected the 15 most interesting cases for *Life After Near Death*. In the process, I spoke with hospice nurses, chaplains, and scientists, as well as experiencers from all over the world. I collected near-death experiences, out-of-body experiences, and accounts of after-effects.

Mixed Methods Research

It is my personal opinion that in the science of the future reality will neither be "psychic" nor "physical" but somehow both and somehow neither.

—Wolfgang Pauli, physicist

I decided to make use of mixed methods research, combining qualitative and psi analysis. The purpose of the qualitative approach is to describe and observe—to uncover what happened. Psi is a field concerned with the investigation of metaphysical phenomenon.

Researchers use mixed methods research when one method alone isn't adequate. I understood that the NDE phenomenon eludes explanation and conventional examination so I decided to explore and combine arsenals to cover more potentialities.

Most experiencers will tell you that it is very hard to describe their NDE and that answers elude them. I realized the experiencer was only capable of answering in an interview or questionnaire what they remembered from their experience. As a result, their answers would be limited. Yet, what if there were other issues and circumstances that contributed to their experience? Facts and situation that were hidden yet demanded investigation? Was there a way to resolve this? One approach was to ask the questions in a reading.

How Does PSI Work?

I sought to determine how the information could best serve us. As I moved forward to dig up the answers, I arrived at results as astonishing to me as you likely found them. I am convinced that what I received is real, which is why I shared the findings with you. Because I'm not trying to convince you of anything, but only to disperse this information, you can experience this information according to your own discernment.

Although I come to this research from a different angle than most, I think many can still recognize a methodology worth considering in a field that's elusive. So I rolled my sleeves up, put on my research cap, and began the process.

What Does a Session Involve?

A psychic reading or session is an attempt to discern information through heightened perceptive abilities. The information comes to me through a process that involves entering a state of higher consciousness. I ask questions and "listen" for the answers. I then transmit the answers to the client, or in this case, the experiencer. The readings were all recorded.

This is how I work.

I begin by clearing my mind. I let go of all sensations and clutter in my space and physical body. I take a few deep clearing breathes, similar to entering a meditative state. In fact, it is a type of meditative state that I enter. Because of my abilities, I'm able to reach higher levels in this state, which allows me to access other information. I should mention that while I am in this state, I am also completely present. I can tell my cats to get off my kitchen table or glance up at the news on CNN. It is a state of complete concentration, yet I am completely open to receive information. I listen closely so that I can transmit the information. When I am finished, I shake my hands, perhaps drink some water, or take a walk to clear my system.

This is how it comes to me.

The information comes to me in symbols, images, and sometimes in words, which is clairvoyance. I hear things, which is clairaudience. I am also able to sense and smell and taste, although these abilities are less active in these sessions because the information we are seeking was from the universe, not the material plane. The ability to use physical senses is somewhat less important.

Feedback is sometimes provided by the experiencer throughout the sessions. Sometimes it takes place afterward in follow-up emails and phone calls. During the readings as I transmit information, the experiencer often says, "Yes, I had forgotten about that," or "I never understood that part, so what you are saying fills in the gaps."

For the most part, the information from the readings is set apart in italics throughout this book, helping you identify the information conveyed to and through me. I didn't include entire readings in the chapters, but rather edited them for the pertinent information. I also summarized some information from the readings in the relevant chapter, and I also used certain information in other chapters to confirm patterns.

The Specific Process of Readings for *Life After Near Death*
How did we come up with the questions for the readings?

The questions for the readings were derived after the experiencer filled out a questionnaire, followed by an extensive interview. Usually, after that process, I found existing gaps in our knowledge. These included events that occurred to the experiencer that he or she was unable to explain or couldn't answer by checking off a box. This kind of information could relate to an experiencer's personal history, childhood, and earlier experiences, or some facet of the NDE, such as the darkness he or she encountered or the noises he or she heard. I certainly didn't know the answers to these questions, but I was willing to see what we could discover through a reading.

As patterns began to emerge, additional questions surfaced, and these were incorporated into the readings. The experiencers were also able to ask their own questions in the sessions. The most common questions concerned the need to better understand the meaning of the darkness they encountered or the beings they met. Another frequent question related to why they were given so much information but hadn't remembered it all when they returned. Mission was also paramount for most experiencers.

In practical terms, if the experiencer was local, I conducted the readings in person. If the experiencer was not local, the readings were conducted over Skype. I recorded, transcribed, and later analyzed all the readings.

As you have seen, patterns emerged about the NDErs backgrounds and upbringings. Patterns about intent and consciousness, about the universe and the meaning of the experience also developed, which I expanded on in chapters 16 and 17.

✳ Chapter Notes ✳

Chapter 4
1. As quoted in Pollan, "The Trip Treatment," on the topic of therapeutic possibilities of mystical experiences.

Chapter 8
1. Atwater, *Children of the New Millennium*.
2. Christian, *Marital Satisfaction and Stability*.
3. Knoblach and Schmied. "Different Kinds of Near-Death Experience."
4. Perera et al. conducted a telephone survey in 2005 of a representative sample of the Australian population, as part of the Roy Morgan Catibus Survey.

Chapter 9
1. *www.nderf.org/NDERF/Research/number_nde_use.htm* and an estimate based on the 1992 poll.

Chapter 11
1. Omni Publications International, 1997.
2. "Mereon as an Archetypal Solution to the 'Theory of Everything," *near-death.com*

Chapter 14
1. Voss, Ursula, Romain Holzmann, Allan Hobson, Walter Paulus, Judith Koppehele-Gossel, Ansgar Klimke, and Michael A Nitsche, "Induction of Self Awareness in Dreams Through Frontal Low Current Stimulation of Gamma Activity, *Nature Neuroscience 17* (2014): 810–812.

2. Borjigin, Jimo, UnCheol Lee, Tiecheng Liu, Dinesh Pal, Sean Huff, Daniel Klarr, Jennifer Sloboda, Jason Hernandez, Michael M. Wang, and George A. Mashour (departments of molecular and integrative physiology, neurology, and anesthesiology, and neuroscience graduate program, University of Michigan, Ann Arbor, Michigan; and Veterans Administration, Ann Arbor, Michigan) "Surge of Neurophysiological Coherence and Connectivity in the Dying Brain," edited by Solomon H. Snyder, The Johns Hopkins University School of Medicine, Baltimore, Maryland. Approved July 9, 2013. Received for review May 2, 2013.

Chapter 16

1. Pew, *The Significance of the Near-Death Experience.*
2. Ibid.
3. Baruši, "Speculation."
4. Radin, *The Conscious Universe.*
5. Baruši, "Characteristics of Consciousness."
6. Chalmers, "Consciousness and its Place."
7. Baruši, "Speculation."
8. Fodor, "The Mind Doesn't Work."
9. Sheldrake, "Morphic Resonance and Morphic Fields."
10. Jung, *Synchronicity.*
11. Langer, *Mindfulness.*

Chapter 18

1. Britton and Bootzin, "Near-Death Experiences and the Temporal Lobe."
2. Borjigin, "Electrical Signatures of Consciousness in the Dying Brain."

Appendix A

1. Moody, Raymond. *Paranormal: My Life in Pursuit of the Afterlife* (HarperOne, 2013).
2. Du Monchaux, Pierre-Jean (1733–1766), *www.livescience.com/46993-oldest-medical-report-of-near-death-experience.html.* According to *Live Science News*, the report was written around 1740 by Pierre-Jean du Monchaux, a French military physician, in his book called *Anecdotes de Médecine.*

✳ *Glossary* ✳

Afterlife
A continuation of existence after death.

Astral Body
The spiritual counterpart to our physical body. An energetic double lightly attached to the physical body.

Aura
A subtle energy field emitted from and surrounding a person. It is said that all living things possess an aura. The aura can be perceived as a body of light.

Chakras
Energetic centers of spiritual power in the body, as explained and described by Hindu and Yogic traditions. Chakras are not part of the physical body but are part of the subtle energy body.

Channel
A person who is a transmitter of communication between the spirit realm and the earthly realm. They may also be referred to as "mediums."

Consciousness
The state of being or awareness characterized by sensations, feeling, and altered states of awareness beyond our cognizant awareness.

Energy
The metaphysics/substance of the spiritual realm that creates a type of life force that is immeasurable.

Experiencer
An individual who has had a near-death experience.

Frequency
The pulsation at which everything in the universe resonates.

Life Force

That invisible power that connects to everything in the universe, from the smallest molecules to the cosmos and galaxies.

Medium

An individual with the ability to receive information from spirits in the form of the deceased. Information is received in the form of auditory, visual, or somatic perceptions.

Metaphysical

A realm that cannot be seen and is invisible but is thought to exist. A realm that transcends material reality.

Mystic

A person who seeks reflection in a spiritual existence.

New Age

An alternative approach to traditional medicine, culture, spirituality, religion, or philosophy. The term developed in Western nations in the early 1970s.

Out-of-Body Experience

The sensation of floating outside one's body and observing oneself from an external perspective.

Psi

The term to refer to types of psychic phenomena that cannot be explained by physical principles.

Psychic

A person with heightened abilities and faculties that allows them to access information outside of ordinary reality, involving telepathy and clairvoyance.

Reading

An attempt to discern information through the use of heightened abilities from the metaphysical realm. These abilities include clairvoyance (vision), clairaudience (hearing), clairsentinece (feeling), claircognisance (knowing), and clairgustance (taste).

Shaman

A person in the tribal world who acts as an intermediary between the supernatural and the natural world. Shamans may have healing, psychic, magical, and divination abilities.

Silver Cord or Cord
The life thread of link between the physical body and the higher self or mental body. A silver-colored, slender cord thought to attach the etheric body to one's physical body.

Spirit
A non-physical entity that governs the metaphysical realm and communicates through a channel or medium on earth.

Spiritual Sessions
A psychic or mediumship interchange between the channeler, Spirit, and an individual.

Telepathy
Communicating beyond physical means from the mind of one individual to another.

Vibration
The rate at which the energy of the universe moves.

✳ Bibliography ✳

"A Guide to Holistic Healing, Body Frequencies," *www.holistic-mindbody-healing.com/brain-wave-frequency.html*.

"5 Types of Brain Waves Frequencies: Gamma, Beta, Alpha, Theta, Delta," Mental Health Daily, *http://mentalhealthdaily.com/2014/04/15/5-types-of-brain-waves-frequencies-gamma-beta-alpha-theta-delta/*.

Atalay, Bulent. *Math and the Mona Lisa: The Art and Science of Leonardo da Vinci* (Smithsonian Books, 2011).

Atwater, P.M.H. *Children of the New Millennium* (Three Rivers Press, 1999).

Bahn, Paul. *The Cambridge Illustrated History of Prehistoric Art* (Cambridge University Press, 1998).

Bahn, P., and J. Vertut. *Journey Through the Ice Age* (Berkeley, Los Angeles, California: University of California Press, 1997).

Baruss, Imants, PhD. "Characteristics of Consciousness in Collapse-Type Quantum Mind Theories," *Journal of Mind and Behavior 29 (3)* (2008).

———. "Contemporary Issues Concerning the Scientific Study of Consciousness," *Anthropology of Consciousness* (July 1992).

———. "Speculations About the Direct Effects of Intention on Physical Manifestation," *Journal of Cosmology* (2009).

Beauregard, Mario, PhD; Gary E. Schwartz, PhD; Lisa Miller, PhD; Larry Dossey, MD; Alexander Moreira-Almeida, MD, PhD; Marilyn Schlitz, PhD; Rupert Sheldrake, PhD; and Charles Tart, PhD. "Manifesto for a Post-Materialist Science," *Explore, The Journal of Science and Healing 10(5)* September/October 2014.

Beauregard, Mario, PhD. *Brain Wars: The Scientific Battle Over the Existence of the Mind and the Proof That Will Change the Way We Live Our Lives* (HarperOne, 2013).

Bednarik, Robert. "The Nature of Australian Pleistocene Rock Art." IFRAO Congress, September 2010 (symposium).

———. *Rock Art Science: The Scientific Study of Palaeoart* (New Delhi: Aryan Books International, 2007).

Bergland, Christopher. "Alpha Brain Waves Boost Creativity and Reduce Depression," *Psychology Today www.psychologytoday.com/blog/the-athletes-way/201504/alpha-brain-waves-boost-creativity-and-reduce-depression,* April, 2015.

Borjigin, Jimo, PhD. "Electrical Signatures of Consciousness in the Dying Brain," Proceedings of the National Academy of Sciences, the University of Michigan, August, 2013.

"Brainwave Entrainment to External Rhythmic Stimuli: Interdisciplinary Research and Clinical Perspectives," Stanford Center for Computer Research in Music and Acoustics, May 13, 2006.

"Brainwaves and Consciousness," *www.hirnwellen-und-bewusstsein.de/brainwaves_1.html.*

Britton, Willoughby, and Richard Bootzin. "Near-Death Experiences and the Temporal Lobe," University of Arizona, Department of Psychology, 2004.

Bukhman, E.V., S.G. Gershman, V.D. Svet, and G.N. Yakovenko. "Spectral Analysis of Acoustic Vibrations on the Surface of the Human Body," Andreev Acoustics Institute, Russian Academy of Sciences, ul. Shvernika 4,Moscow, 117036 Russia_1993, *www.zainea.com/humanvibrations.htm.*

Cahn, B. Rael, and John Polich. "Meditation States and Traits: EEG, ERP, and Neuroimaging Studies,"
The American Psychological Association Vol. 132, No. 2 (2006).

Cahn, B. Rael, Arnaud Delorme, and John Polich. "Occipital Gamma Activation During Vipassana Meditation," U.S. National Library of Medicine National Institutes of Health, 2009.

Chalmers, David. "Consciousness and its Place in Nature." In: S. Stich and F. Warfield (eds.), *The Blackwell Guide to Philosophy of Mind*, 2003.

Christian, Sandra Rozen, MEd. *Marital Satisfaction and Stability Following a Near-Death Experience of One of the Marital Partners* (University of North Texas, 2005).

"The Close Reading of Poetry," University of Victoria, British Columbia, *http://web.uvic.ca/~englblog/closereading/?page_id=122.*

Daw, Nigel. *How Vision Works: The Physiological Mechanisms Behind What We See* (Oxford University Press, 2012).

Errede, Steven. "The Human Ear: Hearing, Sound Intensity and Loudness Levels,"

https://courses.physics.illinois.edu/phys406/lecture_notes/p406pom_lecture_ notes/p406pom_lect5.pdf. Department of Physics, University of Illinois at Urbana-Champaign, Illinois, 2002–2015.

"Everything in Life Is Vibration," Altered States, *http://altered-states.net/ barry/newsletter463.*

Fodor, Jerry. *The Mind Doesn't Work That Way: The Scope and Limits of Computational Psychology* (Cambridge, Mass.: MIT Press, 2000).

Foster, KR. "Thermal and Nonthermal Mechanisms of Interaction of Radio-Frequency Energy With Biological Systems," *IEEE Transactions on Plasma Science Vol. 28, No. 1* (February 2000).

Fraccaso, Cheryl. "Electromagnetic Aftereffects of Near Death Experiences," *Journal of Transpersonal Research* (2012).

Freeman, Lyn, PhD. *Mosby's Complementary & Alternative Medicine: A Research-Based Approach* (Elsevier Health Sciences, 2008).

Gilmore, Grover C. "Age Effects in Coding Tasks: Componential Analysis and Test of the Sensory Deficit Hypothesis," *Psychology and Aging* (2006).

Goodman, R., and M. Blank. "Insights Into Electromagnetic Interaction Mechanisms," *Journal of Cellular Physiology* (2002).

Greyson, Bruce, Janice Miner-Holden, and Debbie James. *The Handbook of Near-Death Experiences: Thirty Years of Investigation* (Praeger, 2009).

Guthrie, Russell Dale. *The Nature of Paleolithic Art* (University of Chicago Press, 2005).

"The Harp," Iowa State University, *www.music.iastate.edu/antiqua/harp. htm.*

"The Harp Blog," *www.celticharper.com/harpblog/*.

"Harp Therapy at the Bedside," *Harp Therapy Journal, www. harptherapyjournal.com/*.

Henderson, Tom. "The Anatomy of the Eye," The Physics Classroom, July 2011.

Henshilwood, C.S., et al. "Emergence of Modern Human Behaviour: Middle Stone Age Engravings from South Africa," *Science 295 (5558)*.

"How Do We Hear," National Institute of Health, National Institute on Deafness and Other Communication, April 2014.

"How Hearing Works," Hearing Health Foundation (New York, New York) *http://hearinghealthfoundation.org/how-hearing-works*.

"How the Power of Frequency Can Heal Disease," *Conscious Life News*, December 2012, *http://consciouslifenews.com/ power-frequency-heal-diseases/1144786*.

"How Vision Works," *Brain Fitness News* (Posit Science, San Francisco, California), *www.brainhq.com/brain-resources/brain-facts-myths/ how-vision-works*.

"How We Hear," University of South Carolina, *www.sc.edu/ehs/modules/ Noise/hearing.htm*.

"How We See," NIH National Eye Institute, National Institute of Health, Information Office (Bethesda, Maryland), *https://nei.nih.gov/ healthyeyes/howwesee*.

Hrushovski, Benjamin. "The Meaning of Sound Patterns in Poetry: An Interaction Theory. *Hyperphysics.phy-astr.gsu.edu/hbase/mod3/html*.

Inan, Omar. "Interactions of Electromagnetic Waves With Biological Tissues," Stanford University, 2005.

Jung, Carl. *Synchronicity: An Acausal Connecting Principle* (1952).

Knoblach, H., and I. Schmied. "Different Kinds of Near-Death Experience: A Report on a Survey of Near-Death Experiences in Germany," *Journal of Near-Death Studies 20(1)* (2001): 15–29.

Kotsos, Tania. "Brain Waves and the Deeper States of Consciousness," *www.mind-your-reality.com/brain_waves.html*.

Langer, Elllen. *Mindfulness* (Da Capo Lifelong Books, 2014).

Liou, Stephanie. "Meditation and HD," Stanford University, 2010.

Livio, Mario. *The Golden Ratio: The Story of PHI, the Worlds Most Astonishing Number* (Broadway Books, 2008).

Long, Jeffrey, and Paul Perry. *Evidence of the Afterlife: The Science of Near-Death Experiences* (HarperCollins Publishers, 2009).

Mackintosh, Nicholas. *IQ and Human Intelligence* (Oxford University Press, 2011).

"Magic Sounds of Peru's Ancient Chavín de Huántar," *Popular Archeology* (February 2012).

Massoudian Nouri, Farnoosh, MEd, LPC-S, "Electromagnetic Aftereffects of Near Death Experiences," University of North Texas, 2008.

"Meet Your Brainwaves—Introducing Alpha, Beta, Theta, Delta, and Gamma," *www.finerminds.com/mind-power/brain-waves/*.

Moody, Raymond, MD, PhD. *Life After Life* (HarperCollins, 1975).

Muzzolini, A. "New Data in Saharan Rock Art 1995–1999." In P. Bahn and A. Fossati, *Rock Art Studies: News of the World* (Oxbow Books, 2003).

Nave, C.R. "The Interaction of Radiation with Matter/HyperPhysics," Georgia State University, Department of Physics and Astronomy, 2014.

"New Age Music," Sam Houston State University School of Music, Huntsville, Texas.

Oghalai, John S., MD. "Hearing and Hair Cells," Department of Otolaryngology & Communicative Sciences, Baylor College of Medicine, Houston, Texas, December 1997.

Pappas, Stephanie. "Sound Illusions: Eerie Echoes May Have Inspired Prehistoric Cave Art," *Live Science* (October 2014).

Petroff, PhD, Emily. "Cosmic Radio Burst Caught Red-Handed," Swindburne University of Technology, January 2015.

Pew, Alan. "The Significance of the Near-Death Experience in Western Cultural Traditions," California State University, 1999.

"The Poet as Shaman: Language, Nature, and Art in Transformation." *The Waters of Hermes: A Journal of Poetry, Imagination and Traditional Wisdom Vol. 4* (2004), *www.academia.edu/3171431/The_Poet_as_Shaman_Language_Nature_ and_Art_in_Transformation_*.

Pollan, Michael, "The Trip Treatment," *The New Yorker* (February 1, 2015).

Press, Lily Ann Cascio, "From Iconography to Opacity: The Harp's Mythological Origins And Modern Neglect," Haverford College, April 23, 2009.

Radin, Dean, *The Conscious Universe: The Scientific Truth of Psychic Phenomena* (HarperCollins, 2010).

Reimer, David. *Count Like an Egyptian: A Hands-on Introduction to Ancient Mathematics* (Princeton University Press, 2014).

Ring, Kenneth, PhD. *Heading Toward Omega: In Search of the Meaning of the Near-Death Experience* (Harper Perennial, 1986).

Ring, Kenneth, PhD, B.S. Rosing, and J. Christopher. "The Omega Project: An Empirical Study of the NDE-Prone Personality," *Journal of Near Death Studies* (1980).

Rogers, Buck. "The Bizarre Electromagnetic Aftereffects of Near Death Experiences," *Waking Times* (November 2014).

"Roman Jakobson: Language and Poetry," Duke University Press, *Poetics Today Vol. 2, No. 1a,* (Autumn 1980).

Rubik, Beverly, PhD. "Measurement of the Human Biofield and other Energetic Instruments," Foundation for Alternative and Integrative Medicine.

Schwan, H.P. "Dielectric Properties of Biological Tissue and Biophysical Mechanisms of Electromagnetic-Field Interaction," Department of Bioengineering/D3, University of Pennsylvania, July 2009.

Sheehy Hoover, Joanne. "Making Prehistoric Music," National Park Service, U.S. Department of the Interior Archeology Program, American Archaeology, Winter 2004–2005.

Sheldrake, Rupert. "Morphic Resonance and Morphic Fields: An Introduction," February 2005, *www.sheldrake.org/Articles&Papers/papers/morphic/morphic_intro.html*.

Sheldrake, Rupert. *The Presence of the Past: Morphic Resonance and the Memory of Nature* (Park Street Press, 2012).

Skinner, Stephen. *Sacred Geometry Deciphering the Code* (Sterling, 2009).

"Sound Devices Used in Poetry," Santa Monica College, *http://homepage.smc.edu/meeks_christopher/SOUND%20DEVICES%20 USED%20IN%20POETRY.htm.*

Steiner, Rudolf. *The Fourth Dimension (Sacred Geometry, Alchemy and Mathematics)* (Anthroposophic Press, 2001).

White, Randall. *Prehistoric Art. The Symbolic Journey of Humankind* (New York: Harry N. Abrams, 2003).

Whitley, David. *Introduction to Rock Art Research* (Walnut Creek, Calif., Left Coast Press, 2005).

Williams, Brian. "A Glimpse into the Meditating Brain," University of New Mexico, 2009.

Wisc, Anna. *The High-Performance Mind* (Tarcher, 1997).

Valladas, H., et al. "Evolution of Prehistoric Cave Art," *Nature 413* (2001): 479.

☀ *About the Author* ☀

D EBRA DIAMOND is a former Wall Street money manager and artist who left a high-profile life to pursue one of purpose and spirituality. In 2008, she had a transformational experience that left her with unconventional powers as a clairvoyant and medium. As an investment professional, Debra was a professor at Johns Hopkins University and a regular commentator on CNBC. She was profiled in the *Wall Street Journal, Forbes*, the *Washington Post*, the *San Francisco Chronicle*, and the *Baltimore Sun*. She has an MBA from George Washington University and is a graduate of Christie's Education and the Jung Institute. The mother of three sons, Debra splits her time between Taos, New Mexico, and the East Coast. She can be reached through her Website (*www.DebraDiamondAuthor.com*) or her Facebook page (*www.facebook.com/LifeAfterNearDeath*).